Persuasive Online Copywriting

How to Take Your Words to the Bank

Bryan Eisenberg
Jeffrey Eisenberg
Lisa T. Davis

Wizard Academy Press
Austin, Texas

Persuasive Online Copywriting: How to Take Your Words to the Bank

International Standard Book Number: 0-9714769-9-3

Library of Congress Control Number: 2002112746

Printed and bound by Malloy Lithographing, Inc.
Book design and layout by Lisa T. Davis
Cover design by LEED

First printing: October 2002

More Praise for *Persuasive Online Copywriting*

"Worth reading no matter what your role in copywriting for the Web. Great tips for creative copywriting techniques specifically tailored to the online experience."

Debbie Weil
WordBiz Report

"The online marketing industry of today is finally ready to meet the demanding needs of effective copywriting. By reading and utilizing *Persuasive Online Copywriting*, any online marketer can meet and exceed their goals of effectively communicating and persuading an audience to take action."

Ben Isaacson
Executive Director, Association for Interactive Marketing

"Every online marketer should have a copy... to read once and use as a daily reference guide."

Rob Gabel
LowerMyBills.com

"A wonderful, succinct guide that covers both the hows and whys behind creating persuasive copy that appeals to a variety of unique audiences. This book organizes the mishmash of information I know I need and simplifies it in terms I can understand at a glance, offering concrete examples throughout to help those who learn best by demonstration. I keep lots of reference materials – this one is going at the front because I know I'll be referring to it frequently."

Stevie Ann Rinehart
Marketing Communications Copywriter

"What can you do to be heard - and believed - online? Why is writing for the Web different, anyway? This common-sense guide will walk you through creating persuasive, results-oriented online copy, step-by-step. Clear, logical, easy to follow advice for anyone who needs to find and use the right words online, whatever their level of marketing expertise."

Rebecca Lieb
Executive Editor, eCommerce/Marketing Channel
internet.com, a division of Jupitermedia Corp.

"Any businessman or entrepreneur who wants to succeed online should read and implement the tactics and strategies found in this book."

Michael R. Drew
Entrepreneur Press

"Awesome! Chock full of great material for both marketers and writers. And the Afterword alone is worth the price of admission – a delightful case of under-promising and over-delivering. Read this book! Put it under your pillow at night! Get these principles firmly lodged in your chemical memory, 'cause this is the stuff that's gonna make a difference in your bottom line online."

The Grok

For Roy and Penny
who taught us
if it's worth doing at all
it's worth doing wrong

CONTENTS

UNDERSTANDING ONLINE CONVERSION

FOREWORD

This time has been really hard because the press is reporting that this industry is dead. I so believe that access to information is hugely transformative. This industry is not going anywhere.

Maya Draisin
President, Webby Awards
Early 2001

We were at lowest point of the Internet bust when Maya Draisin said it, but I agreed with her then, as I do now, "This industry is not going anywhere." Yes, Internet Marketing is here to stay and it's getting better every day.

And the authors of this book are part of the reason why.

1998-2000: Money fell like rain from heaven and the streets were flooded with stories of teenage millionaires. Those halcyon days were fueled by a mentality that "if you build it, they will come." Investors drunkenly bought into the internet's promise of a "new economy" and billions of dollars were pumped into spec-tech and dotcoms, never to be seen again. But when the investors saw that the 'net's realities didn't quite match up to the glowing promises, investment capital dried up faster than alcohol on a summer sidewalk.

It was during the highest point of Internet frenzy that I published my first and second books, *The Wizard of Ads* and *Secret Formulas of the Wizard of Ads*, both of which became best sellers. But as neither of the books mentioned Internet Marketing, I was constantly being asked, "But what about the Internet?" Throughout the years from 1998 to 2001, my answer never wavered:

"The Internet is a baby born premature. She will certainly survive and grow up to exceed all your expectations, but she must first be given some time to mature. There are some fundamental problems with Internet Marketing that cannot be overcome with simple advances in technology. What internet marketing needs is people who truly understand the fundamentals of human persuasion and can apply them to the internet."

Today it is my extraordinary pleasure to announce that those people have been found.

Jeff and Bryan Eisenberg were talking 'conversion' back when 'eyeballs' were the thing and conversion wasn't even in the lexicon. Their work was greatly accelerated when they added Lisa Davis to the team.

Early 2002: Bryan, Jeffrey and Lisa graduated with honors from Wizard Academy and have since gone on to accomplish a number of internet marketing miracles. Consequently, they were chosen to become adjunct faculty at Wizard Academy, where now they teach the academy's powerful Wizards of Web curriculum. This book contains an extremely important portion of what they teach.

Prepare to be amazed.

Roy H. Williams

ACKNOWLEDGEMENTS

This isn't exactly the book we intended to write. But it's the book that wanted to be written. In fact, given that we've been living and breathing words and conversion for the past four years, it's the book that wrote itself.

But no work is ever entirely the product of one, or even three. This book happened because we persisted. More than that, it happened because many people shared the journey with us.

We owe an enormous intellectual and personal debt to Roy Williams that words, for all their potent magic, will never quite encompass. Philospher, mentor, Wizard and friend, he has been an inextricable part of our thinking from the moment we found his first book and began contemplating the connections between his world of radio and advertising, and our world of Internet sales and marketing.

The force behind any business is the customer, and we have been privileged to work with a number of people, generous of spirit and curious of mind, who were eager to offer their Web sites as crucibles for our ideas. In turn, we have learned much from them.

We'd like to thank our friends, colleagues and advisors: Hal Alpiar, Mark Brownlow, Holly Buchanan, Erin Brenner, Larry Chase, Jason Ciment, Hale Dwoskin, Mitch Fields, Anthony Garcia, Olana Hirsch, Anne Holland, Dan Janal, Laurie Kuntz, Chuck Lickert, Rebecca Lieb, John Morana, Jim Novo, Pamela Parker, Brad Powers, John Quarto-vonTivadar, Dan Roitman, Dean Rotbart, Mike Sack, Bill Schloth, John Simpson, Jared Spool, Danny Sullivan, Corrine Taylor, Juan Guillermo Tornoe, Nick Usborne, John Walsh, Debbie Weil, Allen Weiss, David Weltman and Pennie Williams.

The readers of GrokDotCom and Bryan's ClickZ column have a special place in our hearts.

We acknowledge, individually, our personal debts of gratitude.

Bryan: To my parents, without whose support we would never be here, Stacey for her love and for being willing to wait just another few minutes and Hannah for reminding me of my reason why.

Jeffrey: To my brother, my parents and Cindy for providing the wind beneath my wings.

Lisa: To the Grok, for believing in me. And to Zachary, who possesses an incredible soul, a keen mind, a bottomless heart and is the glue of my life.

Persuasive Online Copywriting

Beginning Words

Your audience is one single reader. I have found that sometimes it helps to pick out one person - a real person you know, or an imagined person - and write to that one.

John Steinbeck

Words are, of course, the most powerful drug used by mankind.

Rudyard Kipling

Writing for the Web. Web word wizardry. Web writing that works. If you've been paying attention to all the publications out there that address this issue, you know (or at least have a hunch) something's different about the way folks communicate in this brave new medium.

It's true. People don't "read" a computer screen the way they read print publications. They don't curl up with their computers for a couple of pages just before dropping off to sleep. And you generally won't find computers on the "reading shelves" of their bathrooms.

That much is obvious. But if you are reading this book, you are probably not concerned with writing that passes for literature or journalism or even entertainment, nor how you might create and optimize that writing for a Web environment.

Your primary concern is writing that persuades and motivates your Web visitors to do business with you.

This is the writing that performs the online equivalent of the conventional sales person: it develops a rapport with your visitors, provides appropriate information, helps your visitors qualify their needs, presents the solutions you can provide based on those needs, assures and inspires confidence, security and trust so your visitors feel good about doing business with you, "asks" for action - all the while keeping your visitors fully engaged in the conversion process.

This is writing that must work hard for you. And it's the writing you cannot farm out to just anyone. You, with your finger on the pulse of marketing and sales, simply must have control. And to effectively manage the quality of your online writing, you need to understand what works, why it works and how to make it work better for you.

Whether or not you happen to be a writer yourself, you must recognize how the writing that appears on your Web site contributes to your ability to achieve your goals of conversion and relevance. Writing that gets in the way of these goals is simply a waste of time, energy and money.

Ron Mayer of InterVideo has written:

> It's interesting how a few words changed or a few sentences moved can make a big difference on what products people look at and choose on a Web site. Unless that messaging is in control of the people with sales responsibility, it's all too easy to have messaging that focuses peoples' attention away from whatever you want them to buy.

That's where this book comes in - it's our plain-spoken, no-nonsense companion to your needs as a marketer working on the World Wide Web. In these pages, we present topical information in a series of essays to help you understand the nature of the demands placed on your online copy and content. We offer frameworks and tactics for creating words that will earn their keep. And we help you understand the nature of the medium, so you'll know exactly how to present those words to best advantage.

Your words are a critical link between you and your visitors; they not only drive action, they contribute to building long-term relationships.

So make them everything they can be!

Writing Considerations

The Importance of Being Relevant

You hear the word all the time. You make decisions based on it everyday.

But do you really know what it means and how to make it work for you when you are trying to get your prospects to take action? Roy H. Williams[1] likes to express it as talking "to the dog, in the language of the dog, about what is in the heart of the dog."

Are we talking about meat? Not exactly. We're talking relevance.

Each and every search engine out there is fighting to be the most relevant. Why? Relevance is in the heart of their customers; relevant results delight their customers. "Bring me what I want, and bring it now" is the attitude their customers bring to the table. So if search engines grapple with the issue of relevance because they know their customers crave it, why do most Web sites fail to recognize and exploit the importance of relevance?

So what is relevance? The *American Heritage Dictionary of the English Language,* Fourth Edition gives three definitions:

1. Pertinence to the matter at hand.
2. Applicability to social issues: a governmental policy lacking relevance.
3. Computer Science. The capability of a search engine or function to retrieve data appropriate to a user's needs.

The third definition is most helpful. To paraphrase: relevance is a measure of how closely search results match the search request.

Relevance is the single most significant factor in getting your prospects to take action.

---

[1] Roy H. Williams, best-selling author and the force behind Williams Marketing, is known as The Wizard of Ads: http://www.wizardacademy.com.

Why is relevance such an important concept for Internet Marketing? The answer to this lies in understanding your prospects and how they reach a buying decision (search engines can be a tool for this).

To persuade your visitor to take action, you must be able to see the world from his or her buying point of view. Ideally, while you maintain your sales perspective, you conduct your sales process so that it is in tune with how customers decide to buy.

We engage in the buying process numerous times a day, whether we are buying a can of soda or making a more complex decision, such as buying a new car. Whenever a customer makes a buying decision, that decision represents the culmination of a process. It may take place almost instantaneously or stretch out over a long period of time. But it's a process, not an event.

No matter how long the process takes, the buying decision always begins when the customer becomes aware of a need or problem. Once the need has been identified, the customer begins to explore possible avenues for meeting the need. This is the important point: the customer searches for a solution he or she perceives as relevant to the need.

While gathering information, the customer refines the buying criteria that will affect the decision to purchase and narrows the field of choice, finally choosing from the best few and then taking action.

The information architecture of your entire Web site must recognize every step of the consumer buying process. Each step feeds and leads to the others in order to create sales momentum.

Selling (used in the broadest sense of encouraging your prospect to take action) is the flip side of buying. Although the sales process ultimately is linear, there are often feedback loops within this process - as there are in the buying process - as the customer reevaluates information. So, it's not unusual to address several, or even all, of the steps of the sales process on a single page.

It is helpful to consider that these processes operate simultaneously on both a micro level (the individual page) and a macro level (the overall experience). You should always acknowledge and address the needs of the buying and selling processes at both levels.

How do we address these issues on a micro and macro level? We'd like to share a tool from the world of offline sales because it is just as, if not more, powerful online. It's known by the acronym "AIDA," or as we apply it, "AIDAS" (Attention, Interest, Desire, Action, and Satisfaction).

Every successful professional sale incorporates these elements; they are the steps that drive the process of turning browsers into buyers.

- Does the page grab your visitors' attention - in about eight seconds? Can visitors perceive the relevance of your page to solving their problem and meeting their need?

- Does the page stimulate their interest and reinforce that they're in the right place? Does it suggest that your solution is among the most relevant and useful?

- Does the page inspire the desire to take the action of clicking deeper toward a purchase? Does it explicitly engage the imagination of your visitors and make them feel they will get value from your solution?

- Is it obvious and easy for your visitors to take that action? Do you ask your visitors to take action? Do you give them relevant information at the point of action so they feel more confident in taking that action?

- After they've clicked, does the next page satisfy your visitors by providing exactly what they wanted exactly how they wanted it?

You must test for and apply the concept of AIDAS on every page of your Web site, not just your home and landing pages. And when you've implemented AIDAS at the micro level of the page, step back and test whether AIDAS is working for you on a macro level.

Are your visitors moving comfortably but irresistibly from your home or landing page, through your entire site, to and through the checkout page?

Relevance is what they want. Are you providing relevance every step towards conversion?

The Message Must Be Meat

Intuitively, you know the words you put on your Web site must leap off the computer screen and cozy up to your visitors as if it were you sitting right there with them. After all, they have a Herculean task: they must perform the myriad functions that a real person would in the real world.

There are many ingredients important to the recipe of writing well for relevance and conversion on the Web.

But before we can tackle techniques, we need to infuse a dose of perspective. Because you can craft the supremest of supreme pieces of writing, and it's going to be utterly worthless if you fail to speak to the dog, in the language of the dog, about what matters to the heart of the dog.

At his Wizard Academy,[2] Roy Williams talks about Pavlov. You remember him, right? He's the fellow who got the dog to salivate to the sound of a bell. Roy uses Pavlov's experiment to illustrate branding and the value of relevance.

You see, Pavlov didn't put an artfully arranged plate of vegetables in front of the dog. What self-respecting carnivore gets juiced about vegetables? Instead, he put down something the dog seriously cared about, something that would get those salivary glands working overtime: meat.

To the heart of the dog, meat reigns supreme. It matters. It's the bottom-line food-truth in the canine world-view. It doesn't matter how fresh those vegetables are or how fancy you dress them up. They'll never get the dog salivating in the first place.

That's what you have to do - identify the "bottom-line food-truth" stuff about your business that's going to perform the equivalent of getting

[2] Wizard Academy: http://www.wizardacademy.com.

your visitors to salivate. What's in the heart of your dogs? What matters most to them?

Only when you've figured out what really matters to your dogs can you effectively persuade them, speaking to them in their language. Only then you can decide how you're going to set the table.

You can write screensful of gorgeous copy. You can pay through the nose to have a first-class copywriter perform verbal magic. But understand this: even mediocre writing that captures the essence of what matters to the dog will out-perform stellar writing that completely misses the mark.

Naturally, you want to ring the best and most brilliant bell you can through your writing. Just keep in mind - if it isn't the meat, the only thing you're really serving up is a plate of they-could-care-less-about-it vegetables.

The Case of Content v. Copy

Not so long ago, Nick Usborne[3] and Ann Handley[4] discussed the apparent distinctions between content and copy, and underscored the critical need for these two forms of writing to function in cooperation in e-commerce.[5] Their message is well worth understanding, because it will help you shape every piece of writing on your Web site so it reinforces your visitors' and your goals.

Folks traditionally consider content and copy distinct entities.

Content is the long stuff: articles, descriptions, white papers, reports. The fine print of your privacy policy. The history of the recorder on a Renaissance music site.

Copy is the stuff that is supposed to motivate your prospects to take action. It's generally shorter and more obviously sales-oriented. Product descriptions to capture attention. Headlines. Calls to action. Assurance messages. Words that aid site navigation and usability.

Content informs. Copy persuades. Seems a convenient way to distinguish the two.

However, when you examine this distinction in terms of your Web site as a system of conversion, the differences begin to evaporate. All the words you create must fuel the persuasive process - from the perspective of your visitor, all copy is content, and all content is copy.

Nick and Ann put it this way:

---

[3] http://www.nickusborne.com. Nick moderates Adventive's I-Copywriting Discussion list and his book, *Net Words: Creating High-Impact Online Copy*, is an excellent reference.

[4] Ann Handley is co-founder and former editor of ClickZ.com.

[5] "Copy & Content: Why They Should Work Together." Nick Usborne and Ann Handley. MarketingProfs.com. http://www.marketingprofs.com/Perspect/usborne19.asp. Permission to use a portion of this article has been granted graciously.

Let's say someone wishes to apply for a grant through a prominent charitable foundation.

That person's purpose on the site is to apply for a grant and get that money to support their cause.

First, he or she will look to the short text, the copy on the home page, in order to find answers to a couple of key questions in her mind. "Am I in the right place, can they help me?" "And if so, what do I do now?"

It's the job of the home page copy to answer these questions, or at least to provide an answer that will compel the visitor to dig a little deeper. And the tone of that copy needs to reflect the broader mission and character of the site.

Once our user decides that this probably is a place through which she can apply for that money, she then starts reading a long page that outlines the conditions of eligibility. This is text that has to be read by each applicant.

If the purpose of the site is to help and facilitate applicants, then the content on that page had better be both informative AND engaging. After all, you want the reader to finish reading this page and move on to the next step in the application process.

In this way, core content takes on some of the characteristics of copy. Content cannot simply be there to passively impart information. Like copy, content also has to be written with a view to the user experience and the usability and performance of the site.

There is little point in a copywriter successfully writing engaging and persuasive text, if the content drags the reader down. And it would be wasteful if the content were magical, only to be undermined by poor copy that was inappropriate in tone and vague in meaning and purpose. Or worse: Both.

So there you have it.

There are clearly still organizational and historical divisions between the creation of copy and content on many sites today. But it's time to break down those barriers.

Those divisions simply reflect the flaws within your own processes, and diminish the quality of the user experience and the ultimate success of your site.

When Content Isn't King

When heavyweights like Forrester Research[6] proclaimed content the single biggest motivation in getting people to log onto the Internet (as well as return to a Web site), folks started jumping on The Content Bandwagon. Fortunately, the rush to pad sites with tons of content persuaded some folks to examine both the role and value of content a lot more critically.

Now that we've got some experience and some data, here's what we know: Not all content is created equal. There are times when content is at best pointless, at worst actually destructive to conversion rates, and in any case most definitely not King (or even Prince).

People do come to the Internet to get content. According to a UCLA study, the Internet now beats out radio, television and magazines as an information resource (only newspapers - by a tiny margin - and books ranked higher).[7] But don't go thinking just because people go online for content, they necessarily want that content from your site or that providing it automatically will help your sales.

Think of it as the online equivalent of the old "milk argument," the one that says 90 percent of the people who go shopping buy milk, so if you want to increase sales in, say, your hardware store, all you have to do is add a milk cooler.

Searching for content is different from going shopping.

When people want content on the Web, they go to sites that specialize in precisely the content they seek. When they want to buy something online, they want sites that offer a simple, trustworthy and streamlined experience. The only content they want is stuff that will directly help

[6] Forrester Research: http://www.forrester.com/home/0,6092,1-0,FF.html.
[7] "UCLA Report Finds Internet Surpasses Television As Key Information Source." Harlan Lebo. 15 August 2000.

them make a more confident buying decision. Anything else only confuses them, or distracts them from buying, or slows the sales process or bloats your site.

In e-commerce, content provides a lot of what you'd get from a real-world salesperson. You've got to have it, and because it occupies a central place in supporting the primary sales goals of your site, you cannot give it secondary consideration in the planning and execution of your site. So make sure you have the content you need - but only the content you need.

You need content that's clear, concise, vivid, compelling, and strictly related to your product or service or to your expertise. It must motivate the shopper directly toward becoming a buyer. These days, folks are even monitoring the effectiveness of their site's content by tracking which elements prompted the best over-all results.[8]

Content is not King when it exists simply for its own sake, or when it attracts unqualified traffic that isn't interested in making a purchase from you, or when it undermines your sales process, or when it adds distracting layers that impede your prospect's momentum toward becoming a buyer. So if you jumped on The Content Bandwagon, consider putting your content on a serious diet. Only then will you find yourself with content that truly rules!

[8] "Optimize Content to Maximize the Bottom Line." Charlie Tarzian, ClickZ, March 30, 2000.

Why Copywriting Online is Different

We're seeing too much stuff online that reads like this: "The blankety-blank is the true essence of a high-performance blankety-blank, delivering sizzling blankety-blank in an absolutely refined way. It's a paradigm shift with profound implications for blankety-blank."

The thing is, your online visitors are 'speaking' very differently. Try this eye-opening exercise: Find a product or service that has user newsgroups, message boards or list-serves and compare how that company talks (pay a call on its Web site) to how its customers talk.

Think creating online copy isn't a whole new ballgame? A while back, we asked Nick Usborne, a gifted professional copywriter and author of *Net Words: Creating High-Impact Online Copy*,[9] to speak to this issue.[10] Here's what he had to say:

> Is copywriting for the Web very different from copywriting for print and broadcast?
>
> Tough question. The incorrect answer is 'No'. The easy answer is 'Yes'. And the best answer is, 'That depends'.
>
> But for the purposes of this chapter, I'll be addressing the 'Yes' answer. It's important to understand why copywriting online is profoundly different from writing for other media - before venturing into those gray, 'That depends' areas.
>
> To really understand why copywriting online is different, you need to step back a little.

---

[9] *Net Words* is a truly exceptional primer on Web writing, and we encourage you to add it to your business bookshelf.
[10] This article appeared in the January 15, 2002 issue of Grokdotcom: http://www.grokdotcom.com.

In the offline world, copywriters work within an environment that was created and is owned and controlled by large media companies and the ad agencies of Madison Avenue.

It's a closed loop. Media companies own the means to get the message out to the public. Corporations buy ad space to reach those people - their prospects and customers. The ad money they spend supports the media companies they depend on.

A key factor here is that the audience has no real means to talk back - beyond an occasional letter to the editor. Offline marketing is a one-way process. Companies use traditional media to broadcast a message, in the hope that multiple impressions will have the desired impact.

This has a huge effect on how copywriters ply their craft. They write in the knowledge that this is a wholly commercial, one-way channel of communication and that success depends on repeated 'hits' or impressions being made on the target audience.

In many ways the offline marketing environment is adversarial. Copywriters are writing 'at' their audience with a view to persuading them to take a particular course of action.

The online marketing environment is profoundly different.

As a 'medium', the Web was not created by and nor is it owned by large corporations. And even those huge media companies online like AOL Time Warner may own a great deal of infrastructure - but they will never own the audience in the way that the media does offline.

The Internet sprang not from Madison Avenue, but from the minds of academics. Long before commerce came to the Web, millions of people were emailing, posting to discussion lists and sharing their views and passions.

Usenet, CompuServe, Prodigy, The Well ... These were all forums within which passionate individuals began to carve out the character of what would later become the Web.

Online, your 'audience' has a huge and vibrant voice. As a 'medium' the Web is quite unlike offline media - it is owned more by its audience than it is by its advertisers and marketers.

People will use email, live chat and discussion groups far more frequently than they log onto an ecommerce site. For tens of millions of people, the Web is more about communicating and sharing than it is about buying.

In addition, the network of the Web has enabled 'consumers' to become much smarter. Sites like epinions.com and planetfeedback.com - plus thousands of niche discussion lists - allow people to share their aggregate experience of online and offline vendors, products and services. They praise some companies and beat up on others.

In the offline advertising environment, such a scenario would be unthinkable. But online, your 'audience' has become an active and vocal participant in the sales and marketing process.

So why is copywriting online different from copywriting offline?

It's because your audience is no longer silent and passive. Online, the audience is vocal, active and connected.

As a copywriter you have to respect that. You need to recognize that. You are no longer writing to single, isolated individuals, sitting passively in front of their TVs or magazines.

You are writing to networked groups of people. That's what makes copywriting online so different, so interesting and so challenging.

Your visitors have the unprecedented ability to talk back and shape your marketing and sales strategies. And they speak to, listen to and hear each other in ways you should heed. It's not a one-way street anymore. That's why the words you put on your Web site and in your emails have to transcend 'brochureware.' They have to be high-impact. They have to connect and explain and persuade AND ignite the imagination.

It's the Customer, Stupid

Ok, Ok, so that's a little aggressive. But really, isn't that the whole deal? Get that part right, and everything else follows. Get it wrong, and, even if everything else is perfect, you'll still fail.

Have you ever been cornered at a party by someone who only talks about himself? Pretty annoying, isn't it? Do you respect that person? Are you comfortable around him? Do you feel such people care about you or what's important to you? Do you even want be there? If you saw that person again, would you be eager to spend even more time with him? Most of us would be looking for the nearest plant to hide behind!

Now ask yourself what was the source of those negative feelings and that avoidance behavior. It wasn't how the person was dressed. It wasn't where the person came from. It wasn't what the person did for a living or who he was with. It was the words.

So let's take a look at the words on your Web site. Are you talking about all the wonderful ways your visitors can benefit from your products or services, or are you talking about all the great features of your products, services, or company? In other words, are you speaking the language of "you," or are you caught up in the language of "we"? (Old joke: Woman comes home from a date. Roommate asks how it went. She replies, "He's an opera singer." "Really?" "Yeah, all night it was 'me-me-me-me-me.'")

The words you use and how you use them tell your visitors where your focus is. Want them to stick around and eventually take the action you want? Then talk about them, their needs, their wants, and how they can get those needs and wants satisfied. Use customer-focused language. Otherwise, they're going to feel like you're the self-centered guest at the party. You may not be, but they have only your words by which to judge you.

Because there wasn't a tool you could use to evaluate the customer focused-ness of your site, we invented one.[11] It's not perfect (there are lots of variables and contingencies, of course). But it has proven to be so useful that it's already gotten a bunch of press.

More importantly, it's already helped a lot of people improve their conversion rates. Link to the tool and play with it before you read on.

As you can see, we parse your page for self-focused words such as "I," "we," "our," and your company name (which functions much like "we"), as well as for customer-focused words such as "you" and "your." Then we calculate several ratios that indicate whether your visitors are likely to perceive you as genuinely focused on them.

The most important is the Customer Focus Ratio (CFR). That's the ratio of customer-focused words to self-focused words. Then you can compare all the CFRs with a complementary set of self-focus ratios. Run the tool to check your site; run it to check a variety of sites. You're likely to have an eye-opening opportunity to see your site through your customer's eyes.

It's fascinating to see how certain sites, and even whole business categories, score. Most sites with splash pages or flash intros score terribly. But what better examples are there of sites pushing what the company wants the visitor to see rather than giving the visitor what he or she came to find? Ad agencies and Web design firms are especially guilty of this!

If you want a rough guideline, there seems to be a clear difference between sites with CFRs of 60 percent and higher, and sites with CFRs below 60 percent. If your site scores 35 percent, know that you have room to improve. But remember: You could score over 60 percent and still have room to improve. Again, it's a guideline.

So test. Test each part of your site. Now look at your text, and make the changes that ensure your visitors feel your only focus is them.

---

[11] The Future Now "We-We" Calculator: http://www.futurenowinc.com/wewe.htm.

Case Study: NewsBios Before & After

With our help, Laurie Kuntz of NewsBios,[12] a journalist profiling service, took the plunge and reevaluated the copy on her home page. Comparing her before and after copy can help you get a handle on how to speak to your prospects about what matters to them. The Grok, offers his commentary:

The Headline

NewsBios has big text that pretty effectively grabs your visual attention when you land on the home page. The old version read:

> We know more, about more journalists, than anyone else in the World.

Yeah? So what! The first thing you want to do to engage your customers is brag about yourself? I don't think so. If you even want a chance to speak to the dog, you'd better give it meat. Laurie's revised version reads:

> Empowering you to know more, about more journalists, than anyone else in the World.

Way cool! "We" is gone, replaced with "Empowering you to" and the entire sense of the headline has changed. If I'm a PR type, I'm all for being empowered. And I absolutely want to know more about it than anyone else in the world, 'cause I'm all for having the inside edge in my business! This headline speaks to me about what matters to me, and I'm far more likely to keep reading.

---

[12] Newsbios: http://www.newsbios.com.

Reading On

Here's the body of the old copy:

> Have you or your clients gotten calls from journalists wanting to interview them? Tried pitching stories to a journalist with no luck?
>
> Let NewsBios give you the tools to educate you and your clients about journalists.
>
> NewsBios is a comprehensive database of the world's most influential journalists. Every in-depth profile is updated prior to its delivery to ensure our clients are getting the latest and most up-to-date information.
>
> We know more, about more journalists, than anyone in the World.
>
> Journalists have two main complaints of the PR/IR industry today.
>
> One, they do not know the beat.
> If you are pitching the editor/managing editor, you do not know the beat. In a survey conducted by our research staff, 8 times out of 10 you should not pitch the editor. If you are, you do not know the beat and you do not know the correct journalist to pitch. NewsBios can help.
>
> Two, Communication professionals do not know the journalist.
> A journalist is more than ink on the paper or the story they write. If a journalist is knocking on your door to interview you or your client, do you think that they have done their homework? You bet they have. Let NewsBios do the homework for you. By learning in-depth information about what the journalist does and who they are.
>
> This priceless tool will save you and your clients' valuable time and money.
>
> Each year NewsBios ranks the Top 100 Business Journalists of the Year, the Business News Luminaries, the Top 30 journalists under

the age of 30, as well as additional publications and events. To find out more about one of these events or advertising and sponsorship opportunities go to our events/publication page.

With NewsBios you get the "picture" on the press.

The opening two questions address potential reasons I - the PR dude - might have come to this site, but these are quickly followed with copy that again touts the wonderfulness of NewsBios. Not an effective value proposition, nor an emotional hook by any stretch. It's simply counterproductive to we-we all over yourself.

Then the copy proceeds to tell me I basically don't know the difference between my head and a hole in the ground. And that's why journalists won't talk to me or write about my business. But NewsBios is the priceless tool that is going to save me.

Wanna guess how a negative pitch affects the dog? Think whack on the snout with a rolled up newspaper.

The revised copy reads as follows:

Are you getting frustrated from sending out press releases to no avail? You have a great story to tell. Your product is unique. Why isn't anyone writing about it? You are purchasing a list of journalists that cover your target beat, but you still are not garnering the coverage your client needs.

Do you want to get more publicity? Are you or your clients getting calls from journalists wanting an interview? This service will provide you with in-depth profiles on journalists you want to reach, or journalists who have contacted you. Know the journalists. Know what they write. It is not news until a journalist says it is news. The journalist has already done their homework on you, now do your homework.

Here is a tool that will educate you and your clients about journalists. Relevant information to bridge the communication gap.
This comprehensive database of journalists profiles span a variety of beats and media outlets. Every in-depth profile is updated prior

to its delivery to ensure our clients are getting the latest and most up-to-date information. A professional team of research journalists is on staff to develop profiles of journalists not currently existing in the proprietary database.

Take time to browse the Journalist Spotlight for a first-hand look at this invaluable tool.

Now this delightfully and immediately treats me like a sentient being and acknowledges the frustrations I might be having doing my job. Not only that, it understands that I have a great story to tell and a unique product. Do I want more publicity? Yeah, baby, bring it on! Do I want a "tool that will educate" me? Darn tootin'! Do I want help with my home-work? Make it easier for me!!

The copy is also shorter. And if you can achieve the goal more effec-tively in fewer words, that's a very good thing.

Other improvements

Laurie employed a few other tactics in her copy that will help keep her dogs engaged in her persuasion process. The revision includes links embedded in the text - each a call to action - that can help visitors move further into the site based on the information they want next.

She also has employed text bolding so those cut-to-the-chase per-sonality types can get the entire sense of the home page by skimming. If you just read the bolded bits, you get:

You have a great story to tell. Your product is unique. Get more public-ity from journalists? Tool that will educate you and your clients. This comprehensive database is updated ensure our clients are getting the latest information.

Not a perfect read, but it gets the point across quickly and effi-ciently. Benefit, service. Aimed at the heart of the dog.

The point here is not that Laurie wrote perfect copy; it is that she ditched self-serving copy in favor of speaking to her prospects' needs in a way that communicates the value of doing business with NewsBios. And that is already getting Laurie more business!

Finding Your Voice: Applying Emily

Every now and again we need to take a step back from the microscope we keep trained on the detaily specifics of designing for conversion and consider the broader picture. And it's actually the picture itself, the image, that has captured our fancy today.

In *Secret Formulas of the Wizard of Ads*, Roy H. Williams presents a little essay that opens like this:

> Born into a wealthy family in 1830, Emily has her photograph taken at the age of eighteen, then lives a remarkably uneventful life until she quietly passes at the age of fifty-five. It will be the only photograph ever made of her.
>
> Incredibly shy, Emily asks her friends to speak to her through an open door from an adjoining room while she stands behind the wall. Her life consists of tending her garden and baking. She never travels, never marries, and rarely leaves her home. Emily lives in a world of imagination where words are all she requires to generate a series of vivid associations.[13]

Think about this for a minute. The only image lots of folks ever had of Emily (Dickinson, that is) was a static daguerreotype - a woman perpetually eighteen. Of course, she didn't stay eighteen. And the dimensions of her personality no doubt encompassed more than what the photograph suggested. But that photograph and her words defined who Emily was.

---

[13] "Emily Lives Inside Herself." *Secret Formulas of the Wizard of Ads*. Roy H. Williams. Austin: Bard Press. 1999. p 64.

What has this got to do with you? Lots, actually. It's a brilliant metaphor for how you conduct your business on the Web, and the sorts of things you can accomplish if you present the right image - the right personality - through the content and copy on your Web site. We don't mean to sound cavalier, but when push comes to shove out there in cyberspace, who you are is far less important than who your customers imagine you to be.

So let us take you to talk with Emily.

The Importance of Consistency

You're on the other side of that wall, exchanging confidences. Emily sounds understanding and compassionate. But when you come back the next day, she sounds like a gutter snipe. How are you going to feel?

With consistency comes trust. Visitors to your Web site want to know they are interacting with the same, reassuring person every time they come. When you change personalities in the middle of the stream, they get confused. They can't form a coherent image of you.

The Importance of Personality

Who Emily actually is behind that wall matters far less than what she has to say and how she says it. And as you sit there listening to her, who you "see" is actually based on a very limited experience of her. It is through her words that she ignites your imagination and helps you form your image.

In reality, you can be the toast of the party or even a dreadful bore - it really doesn't matter online. What does matter is the character of the personality you create through your words. They are the elements that help construct the image of you that is going to make a huge difference to your visitors.

The Importance of a Relationship

Behind her wall, Emily engages you in conversation, and you never doubt that you have her complete attention. Now, maybe she's really making notations in her gardening diary or deciding which sauce to whip up for the roast beef that night, but that isn't the point. The important thing is, you feel her words are just for you.

That's how you want your visitors to feel - as though you are there for and speaking to them and them alone! Of course your relationship will grow and develop over time.

It all comes down to the importance of words and their power to create the image you must convey to your visitors. Take it from us ... and Emily.

Benefits versus Features

It's straight out of Sales 101. When you want to capture your customers' interest and speak to their felt needs (the things that make them want to buy), you sell the benefits, not the features of your product or service.

A classic example? Take the electric drill. Nobody is going to buy one just so they can have an electric drill. They buy one because they want holes. Clean holes, deep holes, accurate holes, holes in a hurry, holes of many sizes, holes in different materials.

Most folks don't care what the drill is made from or how the circuitry is toggled - they care that it makes holes. They might also care that the drill is light-weight (but spare them a discussion of the space-age aluminum alloy casing), maneuverable, UL approved, has a super-long cord and comes in its own carrying case. But they only care about those things because they add to performance, convenience or safety - benefits, not features, are what appeal at an emotional level.

Or take lipstick. A woman does not care that a tube of lipstick contains tetroboxomanganite hypoperoxidase (we're making this up as we go) - not unless the ingredient itself is a major selling point (think Lycra™).

What is going to grab her interest is that the lipstick makes her look more attractive. And it stays put longer so she doesn't have to keep reapplying it. And it doesn't smear or "kiss off", so she doesn't have to worry about curling up against someone else's shirt.

Less fuss, fewer worries, great look - these are the benefits of this lipstick.

How do you convey benefits most effectively? With great copy. (Yes - a great picture can help, but it can't do the job alone, ever. And it better not be so big it slows the download.)

So look at your copy. Are you selling features or benefits? Are you talking about what the product or service is or how it can make your prospect's life better? If you find you're focusing on features, rewrite your copy to reflect how great that item is going to make your customer feel. Even price matters only when put in the right context.

Consider the value of the product or service to your customer's life, then write killer copy that sells that!

The Power of Emotion

At our office, there's an axiom we keep prominently displayed. We refer to it repeatedly in many of our reports. We constantly remind our clients of its power. There's even talk here we're going to have it tattooed on our foreheads! (We're actually kidding about that part). But the axiom is that important.

Here it is:

People rationalize buying decisions based on facts,
but
People make buying decisions based on feelings.

Trouble is, stuff like this sounds pretty airy-fairy to the procedural business mind (a very rational entity). At least, it does up until the procedural mind gets an eyeful of the bottom line. Still think we're crooning New Age mumbo jumbo?

News Flash! The University of Rochester School of Medicine published a study based on brain activity imaging that reveals emotions are inextricably a part of the decision process. In fact, "if you eliminate the emotional guiding factors, it's impossible [for people] to make decisions in daily life."[14]

Folks with damaged prefrontal lobes - the area of the brain where emotions are processed - are completely stymied when it comes to making personal decisions such as scheduling a doctor's appointment, wearing a seat belt, and yes, even deciding what to buy for themselves!

---

[14] "Rational Decisions Guided by Emotion - Study." Yahoo!News, November 26, 2001.

When humans make personal decisions, they put themselves in the picture and evaluate the emotional risks or benefits of making that decision. If they can't grab onto the emotional image, they can't make the decision.

That's why you ALWAYS have to appeal to emotions. It's why you have to sell benefits over features and decide when you're going to promote style or substance. It's the imperative for writing persuasive copy that creates powerful, evocative mental imagery in your prospects' minds - the sort of imagery that allows them to put themselves center stage. It's why you have to let your visitors know "what's in it for them" and why they should buy from you. It's why you have to woo the dominant personality types of your visitors, employ a selling process that honors their felt needs, offer assistance and assurances.

Emotions. Feelings. The whole shooting match when it comes to conversion. Care to tap into that goldmine now?

Writing Techniques

Speaking Persuasively to One

> *No, sir, I'm not saying that charming, witty and warm copy won't sell. I'm just saying I've seen thousands of charming, witty campaigns that didn't sell.*
>
> Rosser Reeves

You are ready to tackle the heart of the matter: putting pen to paper or fingertips to keyboard. The time to start digging into the tactics of shaping your copy and content is at hand.

The beauty and great appeal of the Internet has always been the opportunity it gives people to initiate, develop and maintain interesting and meaningful relationships, very often with individuals they otherwise might never have known.

The best piece of advice we can possibly give you is to exploit this knowledge fully. When you write, write to one person. If you can make each and every one of your readers feel as though you have written your message solely for them, you will have established the basis for effective communication.

Within the context of this ultimate writing goal, however, you still have many things to consider. While you are speaking to this one person, you are engaging in the art of persuasion. In the words of Roy Williams, "Describe what you want the listener to see, and she will see it. Cause her to imagine taking the action you'd like her to take, and you've brought her much closer to taking the action."[15]

---

[15] *Monday Morning Memo.* Roy H. Williams. http://www.wizardacademy.com.

The Blind Men and the Elephant

It was six men of Indostan
To learning much inclined,
Who went to see the Elephant
(Though all of them were blind),
That each by observation
Might satisfy his mind.

The First approached the Elephant,
And happening to fall
Against his broad and sturdy side,
At once began to bawl:
"God bless me! but the Elephant
Is very like a wall!"

The Second, feeling of the tusk,
Cried, "Ho, what have we here,
So very round and smooth and sharp?
To me 'tis mighty clear
This wonder of an Elephant
Is very like a spear!"

The Third approached the animal,
And happening to take
The squirming trunk within his hands,
Thus boldly up and spake:
"I see," quoth he, "the Elephant
Is very like a snake!"

The Fourth reached out an eager hand,
And felt about the knee.
"What most this wondrous beast is like
Is mighty plain," quoth he;
"'Tis clear enough the Elephant
Is very like a tree!"

The Fifth, who chanced to touch the ear,
Said: "E'en the blindest man
Can tell what this resembles most;
Deny the fact who can,
This marvel of an Elephant
Is very like a fan!"
The Sixth no sooner had begun
About the beast to grope,
Than, seizing on the swinging tail
That fell within his scope,
"I see," quoth he, "the Elephant
Is very like a rope!"

And so these men of Indostan
Disputed loud and long,
Each in his own opinion
Exceeding stiff and strong,
Though each was partly in the right,
And all were in the wrong!

John Godfrey Saxe (1816-1887)[16]

Most online efforts fall short of effective persuasion and are nothing more than one blind man trying to convince another to "see" the elephant as he does. As you speak, you must connect emotionally with your reader, or you will never persuade effectively. You must draw her into the full experience and activate all her senses. You must build for her a whole picture, without which, your efforts at persuasion will be incomplete.

---

[14] Wordfocus.com: http://www.wordfocus.com/word-act-blindmen.html.

Establish a Structure

The key to constructing effective mental images and creating powerful persuasive copy lies in systematic and coherent intentionality. Your copy should not be presented randomly. Instead, it should flow, interconnect, have a consistent personality, and reveal the gestalt as well as the particulars. It can help to follow a fundamental process similar to the one that is used in other developmental or "construction" practices.

We should note that we present this structuring process in an order-dependent, left-brain fashion, but it is entirely possible to rearrange the sequence by allowing the creative juices to do their thing first and then organizing the exuberant results into a structure.

Many copywriters will tap into the emotional ambiance of the message first and then distill the structure from that. Whichever way you come at the task, your result must have a logical, progressive framework that your reader can quickly apprehend and that will propel her through your conversion process.

The concept of wireframing comes from engineering development practice; it is the preliminary phase of development that leads to storyboarding and prototyping. Wireframing takes its name from the skeletal wire structures that underlie any type of sculpture. Without this foundation, there is no support for the fleshing-out that creates the finished piece.

In Web-speak, a wireframe is a skeletal rendering of every click-through possibility on your site - a text-only "action," "decision" or "experience" model. Wireframing attends to the 'what' and 'why' issues of your project; it is not at all concerned with 'how'. Its purpose is to maintain the flow of your specific logical and business functions by identifying all the entry and exit points your users will experience on every page of your site.

The goal is to ensure your needs and the needs of your visitors will be met effectively in the resulting Web site.

You wireframe first, before a single line of code is written, a single graphic or color is chosen, or a single word of copy is composed. Wireframing is not concerned with design, navigational layout, content or even the developers' and designers' concepts of how to produce your Web site.

In the same fashion, you want to wireframe your writing project - plan its flow so you have a template for its construction, an idea of where you will be incorporating calls to action, points of action, headings, navigation, content resources, and so on.

In his copywriting book, Joseph Sugarman presents a straightforward, linear flow - essentially a wireframe - of the process of writing advertising copy that follows a reader's natural progression of interest and concern:

- Open strongly by eliciting interest and excitement
- Develop the drama
- Explain why the product or service is different
- Explain how to use the product or service
- Elaborate on the unique benefits
- Justify the purchase
- Identify the lasting value
- Address service concerns
- Ask for order[17]

By itself, this topical flow appears pretty uninspiring; the craft of writing will convert it into persuasive magic. But it does exactly what it should do: it answers the 'what' and 'why' questions that should frame the structure of your project - what forms of writing do you require and why - and allows you to turn productively to the tactical 'how' questions.

Once you have decided on the structure of your wireframe (and it needn't replicate Joseph Sugarman's example), you begin to storyboard your content. This is where you start to consider the mental images and personality you want to present so you can persuade your reader to take action.

Find all the words that help describe the complete mental images you need to convey - all the nouns that draw the mental picture and all the adjectives that modify these. Then relate these nouns with verbs, which are

[17] *Advertising Secrets of the Written Word : The Ultimate Resource on How to Write Powerful Advertising Copy.* Joseph Sugarman. Delstar Publishers. 1997. p 96.

modified by adverbs. Finally, add prepositions to form complete sentences and paragraphs that will evoke the full mental image and its associations in the mind of the reader.

Alongside your structural elements, jot down phrases that elaborate your images and begin to develop very rough drafts of the central points you will address. Your results at this stage will look a lot like an enhanced flow chart - descriptions of mental imagery joined with the summary of your objectives.

A lot of effort? Perhaps. But if you have no idea where you need to go, how will you ever know you've arrived?

Define a Perspective

You need to make a series of choices about your copy that will serve as writing guidelines. There are truly no right or wrong choices to make here, simply decisions. Each choice provides a framework for unifying your message and defining the boundaries that will allow you to make your point strong and clear. Once you've made a choice, honor the integrity of that perspective and stick with it. If you discover it's the wrong choice for the project, then start afresh. Don't vacillate between the perspectives.

Perspective No. 1: Intellect versus Emotion
Intellectual copy presents new information in an attempt to lead readers to a new conclusion. Emotional copy tells readers what they already know to be true, subtly inserting a new perspective that influences them to feel differently about the information. Before you put pen to paper, you must consciously choose whether your writing is going to appeal at an intellectual or emotional level.

Perspective No. 2: Then versus Now
The past tense speaks of what has already happened. The future tense speaks of what might happen. The present tense speaks of what is happening right now. There is a presence in the present tense; because it places the reader directly in the action, it most effectively engages the brain. But there are times when you need to evoke the experience of the past or the promise of the future. Consider which perspective will give your copy its greatest impact.

Perspective No. 3: Me, Them or You

First person perspective is that of the speaker: I am standing. Second person perspective is that of the reader: The copy starts with "You are standing in the snow, 5 ½ miles above sea level..." Third person perspective is that of the outsider: They are standing. In general, people tend to find first and third person perspectives less engaging. Second person perspective puts you right there in the action - you, the person you care most about. To your readers, it's them. When your goal is to persuade action, the "understood you" is extremely powerful: it's the imperative call to act ("Click here"); it's the avenue that will lead your readers to the richest, most satisfying mental imagery.

Perspective No. 4: Time versus Money

Business owners like to think their products or services are money-driven: "It has always been and it will always be about price." But it's only that way because we think about it that way, because advertising promotes products and services based on price. Yet these days, particularly in the United States, the customer is more often interested in saving time. There are probably a few exceptions to that. If your product saves both time and money, you have to make a choice of which to use in your copy.

Perspective No. 5: Style versus Substance

Are you going to sell style, or are you going to sell substance? It's an important choice. Here's a Rule of Thumb: If your product is mainly about style, you can promote it with style; if your product or the decision to buy the product is mainly about substance, then you'd better promote it with substance.

Do you remember Nissan's GI Joe™, Ken™ and Barbie™ advertisement? It constituted one of the most famous ad campaigns in the last 10 years. Unfortunately Nissan spent over two hundred million dollars on it, and sales actually went down. Very few people make the decision to invest $35,000 in a substance product like a car based solely on style. Nissan learned the hard way; now their ads focus on substance.

Perspective No. 6: Pain versus Gain

Will your copy appeal to your readers' fear of loss or their hope of gain? Experiments show when people are offered a choice between a guaranteed

$3,000 or an 80% chance at $4,000, almost all people choose the sure thing. Hope of gain is motivating when there are no attendant risks. But there is something far more compelling in the fear of loss. However, speaking to pain, igniting the fear of loss, can be dangerous - it can conjure unpleasant mental images. If you choose this path, use it wisely.

Defining perspectives within your Web site requires a bit more constraint than defining perspectives in the various email campaigns you undertake. Particularly in email, where very often your goal is to nurture a long-term relationship with your customer, your messages would become predictable and boring if you always wrote with the same combination of choices.

Your goal is to develop strong, consistent copy that persuades, and you want to maximize the persuasive power of your copy appropriate to the actions you seek to motivate. Invariably, poor copy results when you find yourself halfway down the path before you ever decided which way you really meant to go.

A Cornucopia of Writing Ideas

You won't snag or woo your customers with drabness; you'll woo them with skillful wordsmithing that penetrates their souls, captures their attention and speaks to them. It's nice to have an arsenal of techniques at your disposal that prevents you from writing the same thing the same way every time.

You can fill your shelves with books about writing - we won't presume to recreate every option available to you. But we would like to pique your enthusiasm and get you thinking about how you can infuse your content and copy with appealing creativity.

All the ideas below challenge you to create writing that is memorable and persuasive, to think outside the boxes and color outside the lines. You are out to win the hearts and minds of people who are actively involved in the dynamic, interactive medium of online communication. And that won't happen if your writing is lackluster.

Roy Williams suggests, "If you will illuminate the mind, win the heart, inspire the public, and change the world, steal a few moments each day to quietly walk the path of poetry."[18] When we seek to persuade effectively, we should communicate a new perspective in an economy of words, and few do this better than the poet. "Poetry ... is about unusual combinations of unpredictable words that surprise Broca... gain the voluntary attention of the [reader and persuade him to feel the way we want him to feel]. It is about transferring a new perspective."[19]

Frosting, after Robert Frost, is one of the simplest techniques you can employ to bring light and life to otherwise dull writing. Take what you have

---

[18] *Secret Formulas of the Wizard of Ads.* Roy H. Williams. Austin, Texas: Bard Press. 1999.
[19] *Accidental Magic.* Roy H. Williams. Austin, Texas: Bard Press. 2001. p 18.

written, "and without changing the message structurally, replace all the common, predictable phrases with unexpected, interesting ones."[20] Make word combinations that bring very bright, vivid and unforgettable images to mind.

> To Frost: Replace common, predictable phrases with unexpected, colorful ones.

Frost could have written:
> There are things that can ruin a wall
> Like freezing
> Which makes the top rocks of the wall fall down
> So even two people together can walk through the holes.

Instead, personifying freezing and choosing more unusual words, he wrote:
> Something there is that doesn't love a wall,
> That sends the frozen ground swell under it,
> And spills the upper boulders in the sun;
> And makes gaps even two can pass abreast.[21]

Franking, derived from the photographic style of Robert Frank, requires you to select your details sparingly and use them suggestively rather than blatantly. The critical element in Franking is to choose an unexpected perspective from which you reveal your message, an angle that puts your reader directly in the scene.

When photographing an opera, Frank eschewed the conventional "photo op" locations and took his pictures from the orchestra pit. As the viewer, you are drawn into the thick of the experience and presented with a far more compelling interpretation of a predictable event that engages your interest and excites your imagination. So what intriguing vantage points can you come up with?

> To Frank: Write accurately, select which details to include and which to omit, view the subject from an unusual angle.

[20] *Accidental Magic.* p 18.
[21] "Mending Wall." Robert Frost. Appearing in *The United States in Literature*. Robert C. Pooley, General Editor. Chicago: Scott, Foresman and Company. 1963. p 558.

SINGLE BLACK FEMALE...

Seeks male companionship, ethnicity unimportant.
I'm a svelte good looking girl who LOVES to play. I love long
walks in the woods, riding in your pickup truck, hunting,
camping, and fishing trips, cozy winter nights lying by the fire.
Candlelight dinners will have me eating out of your hand.
Rub me the right way and watch me respond. I'll be at the front
door when you get home from work, wearing only what nature
gave me. Kiss me and I'm yours. Call xxx-xxxx and ask for Daisy.
(Callers - and there were many - got the local animal shelter.
Seems Daisy was a playful black Labrador puppy! Apocryphal
though this story may be - it's made the rounds on the Web - it is
nevertheless a brilliant example of Franking.)

Seussing, named for the mischievous and whimsical Dr. Seuss, engages
your reader by demanding first the attention of the illogical, nonjudgmen-
tal right brain before conquering the rational left hemisphere of the brain.
It emphasizes verbs over nouns and adjectives, and uses unofficial, fanciful
words - the reader instinctively knows their meaning, even though he has
never heard them before. It's not to be over-used; "like pepper sauce ... a
tiny bit adds zip to even the blandest of dishes."[22] But used judiciously, it
can make your copy leap off the page and settle delightfully in your
prospect's brain.

Another writing technique everyone associates with Dr. Seuss is
the use of meter. When words generate their own "beat," they very often
become more appealing and very memorable - the right brain quickly latch-
es on to them and pays attention. Meter makes your words seem that much
more musical. While Dr. Seuss employed different meters in his writing, he
most frequently used the anapest, a rolling meter with a soft-soft-hard
rhythm (the accented syllables appear in bolding):

> On the **end** of a **rope** he lets **down** a tin **pail**
> And you **have** to toss **in** fifteen **cents** and a **nail**
> And the **shell** of a **great**-great-great **grand**father **snail**[23]

---

[22] *Accidental Magic.* p 20.
[23] *The Lorax* (1971). Appearing in *Six by Seuss*. Dr. Seuss (Theodore Geisel). New York:
Random House. 1991. p 290.

To Seuss: Invent new words that the reader intuitively understands the meaning of; use meter.

Being Monet. In 1869 Monet was painting at La Grenouillere when he realized shadows are not just black or brown, but are influenced by their surrounding colors. He further realized the color of an object is modified by the light in which it is seen, by reflections from other objects and by contrast with juxtaposed colors.

Likewise the meaning of the word is influenced by the surrounding words; that's what Frosting is all about. The color of a word is modified by the light in which it is seen, by reflections from words near it and by contrast with words juxtaposed to it. The meaning of a word changes entirely depending upon the words along side it, and depending upon the context in which it is used. Being Monet is to write impressionistically rather than accurately; it's also to use poetic exaggeration and overstatement. You don't have to be accurate to tell the truth; the truth is bigger than the facts. To be Monet is to select emotional words according to the intensity of their associations or colors.

To Monet: Write impressionistically; exaggerate and overstate; choose emotional words for their associations; remove the black words.

A note takes flight, makes to soar sonorous and pure,
the voice of light fashioning ambiance for the soul.
Another and another lift with grace into being,
blending, merging
until voices
contrapuntal, polyphonic, in cadence antique
etch traces of modal musical lace across the landscape of reason.

Music from the Middle Ages
Experience a renaissance.
LadyFingers

Frameline Magnetism is a technique you often see in visual images - it excites the imagination by asking the viewer to fill in what was not pictured.

Pictures have framelines, edges that define the boundaries of the scene. When an object is cropped against the frameline - when a portion of the object is missing from the scene - the imagination fills in the missing parts. The same captivating technique can be used verbally.

> Spider, Spider on the wall.
> Ain't you got no smarts at all?
> Don't you know that wall's fresh plastered?
> Get off that wall, you dirty ... spider.[24]

Left unsaid or unwritten, the missing word is yet communicated. And what is missing lodges that much more memorably in your reader's mind.

Focus on verbs. You pack punch in your writing not with nouns or adjectives or adverbs, but with verbs. Nothing engages or moves your reader like a good verb. Many times, choosing the right word comes down to choosing a verb, or one of its grammatical forms.

"The verb is the heartthrob of a sentence," says Karen Elizabeth Gordon in *The Transitive Vampire*,[25] while Strunk and White, in *Elements of Style* instruct, "Write with nouns and verbs, not with adjectives and adverbs. The adjective hasn't been built that can pull a weak or inaccurate noun out of a tight place [the same can be said of adverbs for verbs]. ... It is nouns and verbs that give to good writing its toughness and character."[26]

One of the most important verb issues you will work with is voice. There are two voices: active and passive. Active voice emphasizes the subject, the agent of the action; passive voice shifts the focus to what is happening, the action itself. As a general rule of thumb, when you want to inspire confidence and motivate someone to take action, you want to use the active voice.

> **Passive**: The mail was delivered in a timely fashion. ("by someone" is implicit, but not stated.)
> **Active**: The postman delivered the mail in a timely fashion.

[24] *Accidental Magic.* p 24.
[25] *The Deluxe Transitive Vampire: The Ultimate Handbook of Grammar for the Innocent, the Eager, and the Doomed.* Karen Elizabeth Gordon. New York: Pantheon Books. 1993. p 40.
[26] *The Elements of Style.* William Strunk, Jr. and E. B. White. Third Edition. Boston: Allyn and Bacon. 1979. p 71.

Passive: The stew was being gobbled by the ravenous crone. ("by someone" is the crone)
Active: The ravenous crone gobbled the stew.

Passive voice has its uses - it is exceptionally good at helping you set a particular mood. But for most sales purposes, it is wordy, vague and distances your customer, very often just when you want to draw them in.

Compare these two descriptions:

Passive Description: Once the button has been clicked, the order is generated immediately and an e-mail confirmation will be sent automatically to you.

Active Description: When you click the button, we immediately generate your order and automatically send you an e-mail confirmation.

See the difference? Feel the difference? The first description is wordier, vague and requires the customer to make some assumptions - who's clicking, who's generating, who's sending. It feels shifty, as if it might actually be lying to you. In contrast, the active description is short and sweet. You do this and we'll do that. Ta-dah! There's comfort in the active voice. You can trust the active voice. It gets things done. It makes promises that don't sound wishy-washy. It's the voice of accountability!

Now think about this:

Passive Description: The Sonic Drill can be used to make holes up to two inches deep and one inch in diameter using the accessory kit that is packaged in the set. Expanded possibilities are made available through additional attachments that can be purchased separately.

Active Description: The Sonic Drill has everything you need to make perfect holes up to two inches deep and one inch in diameter, quickly and easily. We also stock accessories that make it a snap for you to expand your possibilities.

The active description involves your customer and puts her inside the activity. The passive description requires her to work hard to make the product relevant to her. More than that, it simply sounds too pompous to be appealing. One of the greatest attributes of the active voice is that it embraces the individual. And when you can get your customers imagining your words are speaking directly to them, you have their emotional attention and involvement. They are engaged. They are with you in spirit. You are that much closer to persuading them to take action.

Verbs help you out in other ways. Screen space is always at a premium, and good writing doesn't come cheap. Every word costs you something, so you want to make the most of every word you use. Writing with verbs not only gives you a stronger verbal effect, it can often save you space.

Sample 1
I went slowly along the sandy shore. The small, cold waves lazily came on in long, thin fingers of white foam. The sky was slate-gray and blew a thin, humid wind reticently toward the dark beach. (36 words)

Sample 2
I crept close to the shore. The waves limped in and collapsed in dying fingers of foam. The sky brooded, darkened, then persuaded the reticent wind toward the beach. (29 words)

Now read the two samples aloud. Listen to how your voice sounds as you read them. Feel a difference? Do you think one delivers more punch?

Sample 1 feels slow, dull and plodding ... too many modifiers. Sample 2 is crisper, more compelling, more exciting. Not only do verbs and their associated forms generate motion, they also convey character: creeping, limping, collapsing, dying ... all create a strong mental image and mood - mandatory for effective writing. Sample 1 created its mood with ten adjectives and three adverbs; Sample 2 used only two adjectives (and one of those a verb form) and no adverbs, yet achieved a more powerful result.

Mood. Verbs can help communicate meaning and quality in a sentence without bogging down the language with unnecessary modifiers.

We *go* to the store.
We *trudge* to the store.

In both sentences, we arrive at the same place (and in the same number of words), but the second example gives you a much better idea of how we'll get there and what mood we're in.

Verbs as Adjectives. Folks have grammar nightmares when someone mentions participles, but a participle is nothing more than a verb used as an adjective (a word that modifies a noun).

Vanquished by his foe, the commander knelt on the ground. (vanquished commander)
Dripping with rain, the mouse scurried under a toadstool. (dripping mouse)
The *surrendered* document lay on the table. (surrendered document)

Verbs as Nouns. Ditto the nightmare stuff when it comes to gerunds, but gerunds are just verbs with -ing endings that work as nouns.

Giving is better than *receiving*.
His fear is *losing* control.
She adores *listening* to bagpipes.

In all their incarnations, verbs breathe essence and vitality into your writing. By their very nature, they are action-oriented and quickly draw your reader into a powerful mental universe of activity, sound and feeling. They also pull your reader through the text. Verbs are like seductresses with come-hither gestures! Use them well, and you will help keep your reader hooked.

Use Alliteration. Alliteration is the technique of using the same letter (or sound - "ph" sounds like "f") at the beginning of each word in a series. Used sparingly, particularly in subject lines and headings, it can be a clever strategy to capture your reader's attention. A newsletter from an online company specializing in products for people with curly hair created this subject line for one of their newsletters:

Freedom from February's Frizzies[27]

Use Repetition. You can often make a point succinctly and dramatically by using (but not overusing) repetition. It worked very nicely in the television advertisement that went: "This is your brain. This is your brain on drugs."

Repetition of imperative verbs can keep calling the reader back to the main activity, as in this example:

See the cleaner lift out stains.
See the reds get redder, the blues bluer.
See how, without soap or foam ...
See the spick-and-span result.[28]

Develop a Pace. Powerful writing matches its pace to the feeling it intends to create. To inspire an excited, fast-moving feeling in your reader, use punctuation sparingly, and impart motion through the use of action verbs and short, rolling words. If you want to convey a relaxed and sleepy feel, a sense of rest or moodiness, lengthen your sentences, use abundant punctuation, descriptives, and pay very close attention to detail.

Your pulse races, hands clenching your ticket as she comes flying into the homestretch. Whispering a prayer, you watch her cross the line. A photo finish. Too close to call. Eternal silence. Bated breath. The announcement crackles in your ear. She lost. By a nose.

How do you feel? Breathing just a bit shallower?

Your fingers finally uncramp and ease their vise grip on damp paper, a palpable weight in your open palm, the embodiment of hope that has become failed dream. You shred precisely, with contempt, then surrender the useless burden, and the tatters flutter

[27] Curl Friends: http://www.curlfriends.com.
[28] *The Craft of Copywriting*. Alastair Crompton. London: Hutchinson Business. 1987. p 87.

like betrayal to the stained concrete at your feet, no longer distinguishable in their promise from crumpled candy wrappers and empty plastic cups.

Now how do you feel? Can you see the palm opening in slow motion, ticket fragments falling like decayed petals? Can you sense the despair?

Develop a Rhythm. Rhythm is essentially an alternating recurrence of similar elements. Songs have rhythm; jokes have rhythm in their timing and delivery. Good writing has rhythm that is revealed in the variation of sentence length. When you write sentences that are all the same length, your writing develops a plodding predictability. To avoid this, mix up your sentence lengths: a short sentence, a long sentence, a medium sentence, then another short sentence. This sentence will carry some impact, because the reader wasn't expecting it. Another short sentence might reinforce the impact. Then a long one. Give your reader the experience of rhythm in variety.

Interestingly, there is a "rhythm in three." When you incorporate a series of things into a sentence, three seems to be the magic number. It has a nice rhythm. "We load up the car, roll down the windows and head out into the day."[29]

Use Poetic Meter. You create both rhythm and a pace that pulls your reader through your copy - and helps improve the memorability of your copy - when you employ poetic meter. Poetic meter is simply the arrangement of words in a repeating pattern of accented and unaccented syllables; the traditional forms of poetic meter are the iamb, the trochee, the anapest and the dactyl (see the table on page 62).

The iamb is considered the meter most natural to speech - many passages in Shakespeare's plays are composed in iambic pentameter (five iambs per line) - and many sonnet forms employ iambic meter.

Shall **I** com**pare** thee **to** a **sum**mer's **day**?
Thou **art** more **love**ly **and** more **tem**perate:[30]

[29] *Advertising Secrets of the Written Word : The Ultimate Resource on How to Write Powerful Advertising Copy*. Joseph Sugarman. Delstar Publishers. 1997. p 121.
[30] "Sonnet 18." William Shakespeare. Appearing in *A Poem A Day*. Karen McCosker and Nicholas Albery, editors. South Royalton, VT: Steerforth Press. 1999. p 290.

Poetic Meter		
Mnemonic Device The iamb saunters through my book Trochees rush and tumble While the anapest rolls like a babbling brook Dactyls are stately and classical		
Meter Name	**Meter Form** (/ indicates stress)	**Example** (bolding indicates stress)
Iamb	u /	The iamb **saun**ters **through** my **book**
Trochee	/ u	**Tro**chees **rush** and **tum**ble
Anapest	u u /	While the **an**apest **rolls** like a **bab**bling **brook**
Dactyl	/ u u	**Dac**tyls are **state**ly and **clas**sical

Dr. Seuss played magnificently with meter. The earlier example (under Seussing) is written using captivating anapests. The example below uses trochees.

One fish, **two** fish, **red** fish, **blue** fish

Advertising has long taken advantage of the "catchiness" of meter, and the propensity people have for better remembering copy that effectively uses meter.

Winston tastes **good** like a **ci**garette **should**™

Despite the questionable grammar and suitability of cigarettes, the phrase (coupled with a catchy melody), composed of three dactyls and a concluding strong syllable, stuck.

Melts in your **hand, not** in your **mouth**^{TM}

You needn't confine yourself to established metric conventions. The M&Ms slogan doesn't really fit the traditional patterns of poetic meter, but the two phrases are mirrors of accented and unaccented syllables.

Punctuate Intentionally. You want to establish a relationship with your readers; you want them to recognize you as an individual, you want them to be able to sense what you are relating to them.

Therefore, it can be advantageous to develop, and stick to, a standard system of punctuation that has your own personal signature. For example, use commas for brief pauses in speech, ellipses (...) for longer, but still connected pauses, and periods as separating hard stops. Whatever you do, stay consistent and communicate so the reader knows you are the one talking and knows your intentions.

Let's take the former example we used in our discussion of pace and write it this way:

> Your pulse races ... your hand clenches your ticket ... she comes flying into the homestretch. You whisper a prayer ... she crosses the line ... a photo finish ... too close to call ... eternal silence ... bated breath. The announcement crackles in your ear. She lost by a nose.

Feel different? Time is just as collapsed as it was in our earlier example, but it is presented in a fluid way - now you can visualize the event in a softer focus. The montage isn't as stop-and-go; instead it almost flows with a strange quality of suspended motion that is at odds with the obvious speed of what is happening. And simply by changing the punctuation (and a few words). Then, the finality of the event is acknowledged and reflected in the last two sentences: two hard stops.

We wouldn't recommend doing this all over the place - folks lose patience when anything is over-used. But do you see how the identities of these passages differ?

Show, Don't Tell. Be patient, have faith in your ability to put together a credible reality in your reader's mind. Instead of saying "This car is the fastest sports car on the market today," make the reader experience the feeling of maneuvering it ... the cold sensation of the door handle, the whoosh of the leather seats when she jumps in, the roaring of the engine when turned on, the tight turns that satisfy, the way she gets "pushed" against the seat every time her foot touches the accelerator, the tremble of the gear stick in her hand as she prepares for the next shift, the way she attends to the sounds of acceleration, listening for that precise moment when the engine will sing, "Now ... take me to the next level."

Engage the Senses. To hold the attention of your readers, use shapes, colors, and names of things to which they can easily relate and to which they can attach strong, clear mental images. Though distinct to each person, these images do require everyone's active involvement. Mental images are composed of all senses; therefore words like "sweet", "bright", and "smooth" enhance their "visibility". By strengthening your mental images, you'll haul your readers to the places you want them to go.

Be Specific. Specifics are more believable than generalities, and specifics about your products or services are far superior to generalities (or even specifics) about you. Authors of every genre tend to gain your willing suspension of disbelief by means of details. It takes careful attention to describe accurately things you want people to imagine in a certain way. Make each point very clearly; give your readers the respect they deserve as you captivate them by making powerful, relevant, and specific statements about stuff that matters to them - not you - every opportunity you get.

Make it Irresistible. Remember watching a Seinfeld episode, glued to the TV, following several unrelated stories that finally converge into a hilarious, unpredictable, grand finale? It's a kind of template some of the most memorable TV shows have tapped into: a single episode weaves together multiple storylines that eventually connect at the climax. You can tap into this magic as well - it's particularly effective when developed through an email campaign. Alternate between several storylines, lay false trails, add a bit of mystery by withholding some information until the very end of your message. Have your readers need to read what you have to say.

Communicate Emotions and Feelings. People make buying decisions based on feelings. Therefore, it is essential that your reader fully realize the feelings you mean to communicate so she can properly translate throughout your message. Once you have chosen the appropriate emotion to evoke, think of words and phrases you associate with it and incorporate these into your writing. This way you won't just paint pictures, you'll give rides.

Be Provocative. Make your message straightforward enough so receivers are inclined to read it and provocative enough that they choose to read it again. The secret is high Impact Quotient, that is, your message's power not only to convince, but also to enlarge and impress. Readers go back and read the words again when they realize you're writing about something much bigger than they originally suspected. The thought that they have missed "something huge" draws them back to the beginning for a second read. Read a thing twice - even in one sitting - and you've read it twice. You have just doubled the message's frequency.

Be Audacious. Audacity leverages the power of the unexpected. Audacious statements have far more impact than those that are "pre-dictable." Are you avoiding audacity for fear you might offend someone? Are your readers reaching for tissues because you bore them to tears? Go ahead; take a chance worth taking.

Customatix, a customized athletic shoe business, welcomed new accounts with a little audacity:

> Well, you've gone and done it now. By opening a Customatix account, you've just changed the way you're going to buy athletic shoes forever. Be careful. The surgeon general reports that designing your own cool athletic shoes can be highly addictive.[31]

[31] Appearing in *Net Words: Creating High-Impact Online Copy*. Nick Usborne. New York: McGraw-Hill. 2002. p 38.

Think Symbolically. Symbolic thought bridges left-brain and right, the literal to the figurative, concrete realities to abstract concepts. It communicates ideas in such a way that massive, right-brain concepts can be glimpsed on the left-brain's little black & white screen.

Symbolic thought is rich and exciting, satisfying both hemispheres of the brain. It is extremely useful when you try to communicate difficult concepts, and encourages the reader to consider things from different perspectives.

You communicate symbolically when you write in similes and metaphors. A simile is a figure of speech that creates a comparison between two essentially dissimilar things, often introduced with the words "like" or "as." "Cheeks like roses," "lips like wine" and "fog as thick as pea soup" are all similes. The comparison is the reference for the simile.

While there is also a suggestion of likeness between two things in a metaphor, this figure of speech is a bit more complex. In a metaphor, one thing is conceived as representing another thing: a symbol. More broadly, metaphors are "figurative." The example below is rich in metaphor.

Wings
Some only dream of flying
They say you need wings to fly
I say, I have wings
But they can't hear me
I am already there
And the wind is screaming words with me
But I am not dreaming
They say I wish I had wings
I say, you do have wings
The question is:
Where are you hiding them?

A young girl named Piper Loyd wrote this poem and Nike used it in a television ad for shoes - simple copy read against a montage of images. Not the sort of text you might think of juxtaposing with shoes. As a piece of promotional copy, it was brilliant: phenomenally memorable, persuasive, emotional, provocative, audacious, symbolic!

Copy Length. There is a lot of discussion about the length of your copy, and if you believe everything you read, you would only ever generate very short copy. The consensus appears to be that those who read online can't be bothered to read lengthy content or emails, and that long emails, in particular, negatively affect your conversion rates.

Surprisingly, though, shorter copy is not always the better choice.

One consumer software marketer learned this by testing three different sets of copy in an email campaign: A) a tried-and-true version of about three very brief paragraphs; B) a slightly longer version, at about three-quarters of a printed page, that expanded on the offer details; and C) a one-and-a-half-page version that went into more detail on the offer, products, and company.

All three were mailed at the same time in straight text to three equal-sized segments (50,000 names) of the house list. The winner? C. Although it was substantially longer, it garnered a 7.5 percent click-through rate and a 4 percent conversion rate. B placed second with just under 6 percent and 3 percent, respectively.

If you short-change your copy - bleed it of its persuasive power - you can do serious damage to your conversion rates.

All things being equal, short copy is better. We've heard it's possible to make almost any point in 500 words or fewer. We are not suggesting this is a rule to which you must adhere, but it does highlight the challenge of writing well and working some editorial magic. Because if you can say exactly the same thing in fewer words - accomplishing exactly the same goal - that's a very good thing indeed.

But saying less than what needs to be said, just because you've been told copy must be short, is not a good thing. Beware the difference!

You don't want to blather ad nauseum; neither do you want to short change the job. In deciding how much you should say in any situation, be guided by what you need to say to accomplish your goals and meet your customers' needs. Back when the majority of copywriters were men, there was a saying: your copy should be like a woman's skirt - long enough to cover the essentials, but short enough to be interesting.

Your subject and choice of approach determines how long your copy should be. Just remember that copy needn't be short to be effective. It should be as long as it needs to be - not a word more nor less.

The key to writing persuasively and with relevance is to use your imagination in an appealing, different way - a way that jogs the reader from complacency and captures attention. You're not just hawking your wares, you are communicating magic.

Writing "Basic" with a Global Reach

English happens to be the language used by about 80% of all Web sites. We've read somewhere it could be Chinese by the year 2007.

But for now, the *lingua franca* is English. So what do you do if your business has a more global reach, and you have to make sense to non-native readers of English? You write basic!

Now, we make no bones about it. We do *not* generally write basic English, particularly in our newsletter, Grokdotcom. You get us as we are. And that's a perfectly acceptable model - you've got to figure you're never going to appeal to all the folks all the time no matter what you do. Sometimes you choose to "target" your writing.

But some of you out there must communicate effectively on your Web site and in your emails with those for whom English is a second language (ESL). So here's what you do:

Use short sentences
15 to 20 words - and 20 words puts you close to the danger zone. Writing concise, direct sentences is most of the battle.

Use simple sentence constructions
Subject - verb - object (if any), followed by any extra information. You start confusing folks when you insert lots of phrases between the core elements of a sentence.

Use the active voice
When you use passive verbs, you risk making your meaning ambiguous.

Avoid "phrasal" and "modal auxiliary" verbs

Phrasal verbs combine two or more words, as in: *call up, pull in, pick away at* and *put down*. English has about 3000 of these constructions, and they confuse non-native speakers of the language. So choose a one-word verb that says the same thing.

Modal auxiliary verbs include *should, could, can, would, might* and *may*.

A representative should contact you within 48 hours.

Does this mean he will, he might not, he has a moral obligation to or that it could take longer than 48 hours? Native English readers understand these words based on context. They usually perplex ESL readers.

Use pronouns clearly

Notice the last two sentences in the previous section. The "they" in the last sentence refers to a noun in the previous sentence, but which one? Words? Native English "readers"? Or did we make a grammatical mistake and refer in the plural to "context"? See what we mean?

Use simple, common words with clear meanings

Use positive language

Stay away from negative constructions (which can be hard to translate) and negative images (which are depressing and can be insulting). "Don't you just hate it when ..." is a negative construction (don't) with a negative image (hate). Double negatives (as in "not uncommon") are doubly troublesome.

Avoid idioms, clichés and slang

We wrote "make no bones about it." Can you imagine what that means to this audience? Nothing.

Proof very carefully

Writing that is grammatically correct and free of typos is enormously important with this audience! These folks are generally good with English grammar and if you break the rules, you risk confusing them at best and damaging your credibility at worst.

Get some help

If you know people who speak English as a second language, ask them to read your copy for clarity and to help you identify potentially offensive language. This is especially important if you are using humor.

If you want to study a good model for International English, pick up a copy of the Herald Tribune,[32] a newspaper that writes in English for a global audience.

---

[32] Herald Tribune: http://www.iht.com.

Writing for Personalities

From Hippocrates through Jung to Keirsey and beyond, humans have been trying to fathom the dimensions of personality. In the most general scheme of categorization, we've learned that each of the millions of different personalities fall into one of four main groups, which we label as Driver, Amiable, Expressive and Analytical.

It doesn't really matter what you call them. Thing is, you need to become intimately acquainted with these personalities. They are your Web site's visitors. And once you know who they are, you've got the inside track on how you shape your writing to persuade them most effectively.

At the most fundamental level, all people are motivated by a single, critical question: What's In It For Me (WIIFM)? Their dominant personality types strongly influence how they ask that question, perceive value and, consciously - or more typically, subconsciously - approach a decision-making task.

One of your most important objectives is to communicate consistently with each of the four main personality types, so your prospects can "self serve" the information they require to influence their buying decision from the "buffet" of information you provide on your site and in your emails. It is important not only to give people what they want and need, but to give it to them through words that are designed to appeal to them.

On to the introductions! For each personality, we'll give you a general profile, then some specific comments that include the dominant attitude that characterizes this personality, how this personality type typically uses time, the question this personality type is most likely to ask about your product or service and how you should strive to meet the needs of this personality type. Finally, we present sample copy - same copy for each profile, but italics and underlining indicate the language that will appeal most to the personality type.

AMIABLE

Amiables must be authentic. They are always engaged in a personal quest for their unique identity and live their lives as an expression of it. For them, integrity means the unity of inner self with outer expression. These individuals appreciate the personal touch. They like things that are non-threatening and friendly. They dislike dealing with impersonal details and cold hard facts, and are usually quick to reach a decision.

Attitude:	Personal, activity oriented
Using Time:	Undisciplined, fast paced
Question:	Why is your solution best to solve the problem?
Approach:	Address values and provide assurances, credible opinions rather than options

Sample Copy:
Our approach is personalized to meet your objectives. The bottom line is that your results are guaranteed. Explore our methodology to discover how thousands of clients just like you have been delighted.

ANALYTICAL

Analyticals need to be organized to act. For them, task completion is its own reward. These individuals appreciate facts, hard data and information presented in a logical manner as documentation of truth. They enjoy organization and completion of detailed tasks. They do not appreciate the "personal touch" or disorganization.

Attitude:	Businesslike, detail oriented
Using Time:	Disciplined, methodically paced
Question:	How can your solution solve the problem?
Approach:	Provide hard evidence and superior service

Sample Copy:
Our approach is personalized to meet your objectives. The bottom line is that your results are guaranteed. *Explore our methodology* to discover how thousands of clients just like you have been delighted.

EXPRESSIVE

Expressives need to belong. They often feel that they must earn a place by belonging, by being useful, fulfilling responsibilities, being of service, giving to and caring for others instead of receiving from them. These individuals are very creative and entertaining. They enjoy helping others and are particularly fond of socializing. They are usually slow to reach a decision.

Attitude:	Personal, relationship oriented
Using Time:	Undisciplined, slow paced
Question:	Who has used your solution to solve my problem?
Approach:	Offer testimonials and incentives

Sample Copy:
Our approach is personalized to meet your objectives. The bottom line is that your results are guaranteed. Explore our methodology to *discover how thousands of clients just like you have been delighted.*

ASSERTIVE

Assertives seek competence in themselves and others. They want to understand and control life. Driven by curiosity, the Assertive is often preoccupied with learning twenty-four hours a day. These individuals have a deep appreciation for challenges. They enjoy being in control, are goal oriented and are looking for methods for completing tasks. Once their vision is clear, they are usually quick to reach a decision.

Attitude:	Businesslike, power oriented
Using Time:	Disciplined, strategically paced
Question:	What can your solution do for me?
Approach:	Provide options, probabilities and challenges

Sample Copy:
Our approach is personalized to meet your objectives. _The bottom line is that your results are guaranteed_. Explore our methodology to discover how thousands of clients just like you have been delighted.

To further simplify this, we can distill it to its basics:

Amiables focus on language that answers WHY questions.

Analyticals focus on language that answers HOW questions.

Expressives focus on language that answers WHO questions.

Assertives focus on language that answers WHAT questions.

To a greater or lesser degree, depending on the flow of your conversion process, the content and copy on all of your pages needs to speak in these four ways.

Now, a few closing caveats. Humans are amazingly complex creatures, and any classification attempt is a simplification of this complexity. On top of that, no one person is all one personality type. Each of us is a delightful mixture - one type may predominate, but others come into play, often influenced by environmental factors, social factors, even ephemeral moods. So, even though you may know for a fact that 72 percent of your visitors are Analyticals, that doesn't mean you can write solely to the analytical profile. And it's a big reason why we encourage clients to create multiple but interlinking paths in which their visitors can "self-serve" the customer experience they prefer. After all, the Amiable might follow a path that is primarily why-oriented, then decide that to feel completely comfortable taking action, he requires some how-oriented information.

Also, consider the nature of the products or services you offer. Pure impulse-buying is going to appeal most to the friendly, impulsive Amiables.

A site selling engineering equipment is going to attract more Analyticals than Expressives ... and even if an Expressive engineer requires the product, his job requires that he be concerned with a logical, orderly, precise and features-attentive approach.

And if you run an online dating service, no matter how Analytical or Assertive your visitor, she is likely to approach this service in a more Expressive state of mind.

Understanding these profiles allows you to create multiple navigation paths that will be much more meaningful and satisfying to the people who come to your site, because they will appear tailored to their needs. And when you line these paths with intentional copy that appeals to the different qualities people value and the various ways in which they interact with the world, you will be speaking far more persuasively to each and every one of your visitors.

Writing in Review

We've discussed the context of many of these issues. Let's just run through them now, individually, so you can be certain you've covered the basics.

Within the context of the style you have chosen - potentially a very evocative style - are you grammatically and syntactically consistent? You don't have to write in complete sentences. You don't have to use standard punctuation. But it always helps to know how grammar and syntax should be handled, even as you stray from the straight and narrow. And no matter whether you seek to create a more flamboyant impression or write within the confines of corporate tradition, many of your readers will find you less credible and less convincing when you abuse spelling and tense agreement.

If you or your copywriters have been doing your homework, you'll have a pretty good idea how people are talking about businesses, products and services similar to yours. Find ways to echo these styles in your message, from "inflection" to vocabulary choices. You will be much more likely to make positive connections with your audience when you speak to them as they tend to speak.

Always make sure the words and style you adopt are appropriate to the context of your relationship with your readers. Our friend, The Grok, can get away with greeting his readers as "dudes and dudettes," but if you are a loan and finance company or a supplier of serious medical equipment, this might not be in your best interest.

There was a time when people may have expected communications from businesses to individuals to be very formal and proper. And while there may be places where the "Dear Sir or Madam; We deeply regret to inform you that despite our best efforts we have been unable to procure the item you desired" approach might still work, it generally isn't online. Stiff, formal writing feels aloof and distances your reader. Even if formal is necessarily the name of your game, find ways to humanize the tone.

You may reach a phenomenal number of people each month through your online efforts. But when you compose your content and copy, you write as if your only purpose was communication from one individual to one individual: speaker to reader. Nobody wants to feel she is simply a nameless face in the crowd or the online version of "current resident." People don't develop relationships with entities. And when they buy, they much prefer to think they are buying from someone who cares about them, someone who is going to look after their needs.

As you write, picture a specific person. Give that person a character and qualities to which you can relate. Then write to that person, just as you would speak to that person if you were face-to-face. It's interesting to consider that the writing contained in personal letters is often the most engaging writing you can read.

You as an individual and a business have a unique voice, a personality with facets. Use these, embellish upon the conventional. If you sound like everyone else, and *always* sound like everyone else, you are not exactly going to stand out and get noticed.

Keep your writing fresh, unique. Don't overuse clichés, unless you have a specific reason for using them, and don't fall prey to adopting the language that peppers unsolicited commercial mail - particularly in the subject lines of your emails! To confer the broadest appeal on your writing, don't litter it with jargon or insider-speak that may be unfamiliar to some of your readers. If you absolutely must use technology-specific terminology, make it accessible to the lay reader, and pay attention to incorporating the benefits inherent in the features.

Use the passive voice only if you have the perfect application for it. Otherwise, keep your writing voice in the active tense. Your reader should never have to wonder at the implied agent of action. Active voice is much more immediate, more economical in the number of words it uses and inspires confidence.

Skillful use of verbs gives your writing motion, energy and makes it appealing. The verbs you use in your calls to action should be imperatives (*Click* here, *Add* to cart) paired with a clear benefit.

Your goal is to create strong, positive images that impress upon your readers' minds, activate their imaginations and become memorable.

Writing that is suggestive, impressionistic, and that eliminates the obvious encourages more active participation from your readers. Anytime you can get your readers imagining alongside you, you are much more likely to tap into the emotional realm that will persuade both their hearts and their minds.

We did mention earlier that it was important to choose between speaking to the very compelling fear of loss or the less compelling (and more often favored) hope of gain. There are certainly circumstances where fear of loss is the motivating reason for taking action, but if you take this perspective, you must tread the path carefully. Often it is more advantageous to speak to present gain and put the fear of loss in a reflective context. Dredging up distressing mental images is risky; people tend to discard or ignore negativity.

A person should feel fully immersed in the imagery you present. She should be able to place herself inside what is happening and imagine how she would be feeling. Verbs, a second person perspective and language that appeals to the senses are the keys. Remember that to take action, a person must be able to see herself taking that action. Once you have her thinking what it would be like to take a particular action, she is that much closer to doing so.

Stellar writing begs to be read. There is an urgency to the writing that keeps the reader going, even when that reader might be pressed for time. If you can create this sense of drama and momentum in your writing, you stand a much better chance of capturing more of your reader's share of mind.

The Magic Touch of Editing

I'm unable to judge my own work and I don't see how any copy-writer can.

David Ogilvy

You are never done writing. Once you've written, there is the urge to refine. And refine again. Writing can always be improved, but the writer, by virtue of having created the copy, suffers from Inside-the-Bottle Syndrome and sometimes has difficulty reading the label. It's hard to be objective when you've poured yourself into the words.

This is where a good editor makes all the difference. More than simply proofing the copy, an editor can offer the objectivity and skill that turns good writing into brilliant writing. Ego is an unproductive factor in the equation - no matter who is involved in the process, the collective goal is to achieve copy that works hard for you and performs well.

The editor's job is to refine the copy so the fewest words yield the greatest effect, all within the context of the writing style you have chosen. Here are some editorial tips you can use to help improve your copy:

- Look at 'that' words. People tend to overuse the word 'that.' They write "She said that she would come" when they could write "She said she would come." If your sentence makes sense without the 'that' word, exorcise it. One fewer word is a good thing.

- Edit for rhythm. All short, all long, no variation - this gets monotonous. It will bore your reader, who will then proceed to tune out you and your message via the delete or backspace button. Words, phrases, sentences, all have "sound" value; there is an inherent musicality to writing, and a pleasing rhythm will make your writing much stronger and more memorable.

- Consider combining sentences. If you string the same point across multiple sentences, see if you can combine them to make the point more strongly in fewer sentences.

- Remove unnecessary words. In writing, less very often is more. It makes what is there stand out more prominently. If you don't really need a word, take it out.

- Rearrange thoughts so they flow better. There is a logic to the process you are asking your readers to engage in and your writing should reinforce that process. Step 1 usually comes before Step 2.[33]

Writing is a craft; it takes lots of time and lots of practice, and even then, there's always more to learn. Do what you can to tighten and shape your copy, then hand it over to a good editor. Not only will you find you have a better product, you will probably also learn how to improve your technique.

[33] *Advertising Secrets of the Written Word : The Ultimate Resource on How to Write Powerful Advertising Copy.* Joseph Sugarman. Delstar Publishers. 1997. p 104.

Case Study: Max-Effect
Before & After

John Morana of MaxEffect[34] designs ads for the Yellow Pages, and he is a veteran reader of Grokdotcom. He was already doing a number of things reasonably well on his site - in particular, his text was formatted for scanning and skimming, and it included text hyperlinks that appealed to different personality types. But several things were limiting him to one or two leads a week. One of these was the tone of his home page copy.

Old Copy

Eliminate Yellow Page Advertising Hassles Forever
... And watch your calls & sales SKYROCKET !
A Custom Designed Yellow Page Ad by MaxEffect Will:

- Maximize your readership, phone calls & sales... 24 / 7 / 365
- Save you money... Using the most cost-effective sizes & colors
- Save you time... Minimizing YP sales rep calls & DIY struggles
- Eliminate Yellow Pages frustration, doubts & deadline worries
- Nullify your competitors... Letting you dominate your classification

Yellow Pages advertising is expensive, time-consuming and fiercely competitive. A new, custom-designed ad by MaxEffect will let you easily conquer your rivals and save you time, money and the aggravating headaches common with Yellow Pages advertising. Study the following Ad Samples, read a few Testimonials or review our Risk Free Guarantee.

---

[34] Max-Effect: http://www.max-effect.com. For an additional perspective on this case study, see Debbie Weil's WordBiz Report interview with Bryand Eisenberg, "On Before and After Home Page Copy that Engages and Converts Visitors." 30 January 2002.

But whatever you do Place Your Order Now... before your competitors ! MaxEffect clients have asked us, even PAID us, to NOT ACCEPT ORDERS from their competitors. They've learned something you absolutely MUST... A custom-designed Yellow Page ad by MaxEffect is your most powerful weapon when doing battle in the Yellow Pages directory. Your new advertisement will reign supreme.

If you're determined to drive your Yellow Pages ROI to the absolute MAX, you need to Order MaxEffect Now.

As you read this slightly self-serving copy, notice the way the words speak to "pain" and focus heavily on negative associations: eliminate, hassles, minimize, struggles, frustration, doubts, worries, nullify, aggravating headaches, weapons, battle. And on top of everything else, "Yellow Pages advertising is expensive"!

New Copy
Maximize Your Investment!
Place Your Business under the Yellow Page Advertising Spotlight and Listen to Your Phone and Cash Register Sing!
Dare to stand out within your Yellow Pages category!
Then your potential customers will...

- Be drawn to your Yellow Page ad more strongly than anything else on the page.
- Be engaged by your ad so they read it entirely!
- Recognize that you are the solution to what they're searching for.
- Call you, visit you & buy from you!

For just a onetime, low investment you get an express in-depth company evaluation, outstanding graphic design and persuasive creative messaging that will deliver immediate results.

Best of all, your new MaxEffect Yellow Page ad is 100% Guaranteed. Check out some happy clients' ad samples and read about all the business we've generated for businesses like yours.

Contact us now to dramatically increase your sales opportunities!

This shorter revision is more to the point, more believable, completely benefit-oriented and puts everything in a positive light. The value proposition of "saving time and money" has become "making more money." And while "Maximize Your Investment!" is possibly one of the biggest clichés in the book, it reinforces the business name, while the exclamation point echoes the logo. It works for John's customers.

Look and Feel

The other principal problem with John's copy centered on usability issues associated with the look and feel of the site.

The old home page was laid-out attractively, but the color choices made it almost impossible to quickly scan or skim the reverse-color grey type featured on a black background. You could argue it was an aesthetically pleasing color combination, but it played havoc on the reader's eyes.

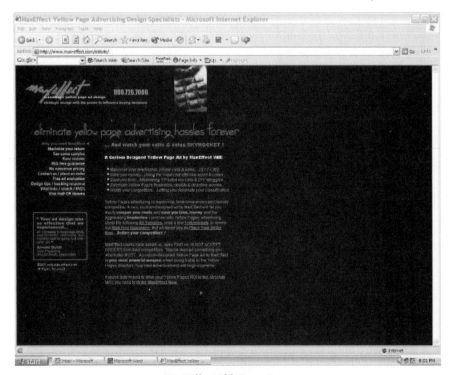

Max Effect Old Home Page

John's Yellow Page ad designs really are distinctive, and he had a sample page of his work. But very few people could be bothered to get past this barbed-wire fence to discover John's skill.

To compliment the positive copy, John needed a positive look and feel, something that was usability-friendly for his copy and, again, didn't reinforce negativity.

The new home page is brighter, conveys energy and, most important, highlights the copy that is critical to John's conversion process: once you've focused on the central headline, you are quickly drawn to text that is benefit-rich and includes hyperlinks as internal calls to action.

With these changes in place, John went from 1 or 2 leads a week to 1 or 2 a day. He got more business than he could handle! So he hired someone to help.

Recently, he raised his rates, hoping that would discourage some of the visitors to his Web site and help him catch up with his workload. It didn't.

What a problem to have!

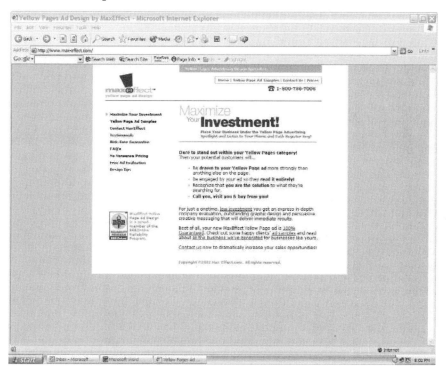

Max Effect New Home Page

The Medium

The Eyes Have It

You pick up a newspaper; your eyes go for the pictures first. So it should follow the same thing will happen when you sit in front of a computer screen, right?

Well, Stanford-Poynter Project researchers discovered that when folks read news online, their eyes went for text first, particularly captions and summaries, and graphics only later.[35] Sometimes much later. Sometimes not at all. This made a lot of commercial writers happy. It also heralded a new phase of inquiry: how do folks scan Web sites for information?

Should you care about this stuff? If you know how folks gather information visually from their browser windows, you've got a powerful design tool you can use right now to support your mission of persuading your visitors to take the action you want.

When a user lands on a Web page, she gives the display a quick scan that starts in the top left of the window, moves quickly across the center to the right, then returns leftward, again crossing center.[36] All this happens in seconds, without the user necessarily fixing her gaze until she reaches the center of the display as she's coming back. It also usually happens without her being aware of it.

She's on a preliminary scouting mission, an effort to quickly orient herself within the context of a page, before she makes the conscious effort to engage with the information.

---

[35] Stanford-Poynter Project: http://www.poynter.org/eyetrack2000/index.htm.
[36] It is important to note that this is the pattern for Western culture. The point is cleverly and interestingly made in "What You See Depends On Where You're From." The Micro Computer Trainer.

How Can I Use This?

- Your logo should be one of the first elements the user encounters at the top of the page (so make sure it's one of the first things that loads). This is your identity, and along with the url, lets your user know where she's landed.

- Global navigation schemes work well here, as do in-site search features (if you use them) - they provide the preliminary assurance of general organization and can serve as back-up.

- Make sure your value proposition is clear and prominent.

Jared Spool's User Interface Engineering group[37] has discovered that a user's gaze ultimately fixes in the center of the screen, then moves left, then right, a pattern of visual fixation that was true of both new and experienced users.[38] A user fixed on areas other than the center only when she was looking for additional information. The team also found users pretty much ignored the bottom of the screen and seemed to interact peripherally with the right area (folks use their scroll bar without obviously looking at it!).

How Can I Use This?

- Clearly the center area of the screen is prime real estate, the "active window" where you will either succeed or fail in persuading your visitor. This is the first place your visitor makes a conscious effort to engage with you. When her gaze returns across the screen from its preliminary sortie, you want to make sure you present content and copy that will capture her interest and motivate her through the conversion process. If anything on the page distracts her or requires her to disconnect from the center area, she is that much less likely to stay rapt in your powers of persuasion. And if you've learned the Stanford-Poynter lesson, you'll understand your words are much more important than your images.

[37] User Interface Engineering: http://www.uie.com.
[38] "Testing Web Sites with Eye-Tracking." Will Schroeder. User Interface Engineering. http://world.std.com/~uieweb/eyetrack1.htm.

- The left side of the screen can function as a "stabilizing window," a place where people look for particular points of reference that can help them locate the items that suit their needs. Comprehensive navigation works well here.

- Even when they remain engaged in the central area, users peripherally attend to the right area. This becomes a valuable space to convey confidence through your assurances, guarantees and testimonials. Calls to Action do well here, too. Notice how Amazon has their Add to Shopping Cart and 1-Click action block in the top right, and below this is their Add to Wish List button. Because the user is peripherally aware of it, she knows it is there if and when she is ready to take that action.

Using this cool eye-tracking stuff, your general order of business is first to orient your visitor, then use your "active window" to keep her attention and persuade her to become a buyer (or subscriber, or whatever your goal is). The other graphic turf on your Web site is no less important to the overall effort, but your users are simply never going to give it the same visual priority.

If you know how folks scan, you have a template for placing things on your Web pages so your visitors will find a) what they are looking for, b) where they expect to find it, c) in the way that engages them best. Don't think of it as limiting your artistic freedom, think of it as knowledge you can use to meet your customers' needs and thereby increase your conversion rate!

Set Up Scanning and Skimming So They See

You spent your time writing right. Not only is your text persuasive, but now you're ready to make sure your reader engages with your text on your Web page.

This, in many ways, is a usability issue.

So how helpful is it when the terms folks use for talking about usability stuff sound different, but seem to mean the same thing? Take scannability and skimmability.

"You mean there's a difference ... and I need to understand it?" you wonder.

You bet! If your visitors can't scan and skim your Web pages quickly and efficiently as soon as they first arrive, they aren't going to stick around to dig deeper. Not good.

Even though these two activities are related, they are distinct experiences in the usability equation and require separate treatment. If you lump scannability and skimmability together, chances are you're going to miss the Usability Boat.

Let's start with the dictionary definitions:[39]

Scan: To look over quickly and systematically (scan the horizon for signs of land), to leaf through hastily.

Skim: To give a quick and superficial reading, scrutiny, or consideration (skim the newspaper).

---

[39] *American Heritage Dictionary of the English Language.* Third Edition. Boston: Houghton Mifflin Company. 1996. pp 1610 and 1691, respectively.

Can you see that they're similar but not quite the same? Both scanning and skimming are information-gathering activities, and humans perform them quickly, usually without thinking about them very much. But they don't work exactly the same way, and they don't serve exactly the same purpose.

Think of it this way: You're on the frontier of the wild and wooly west, and your trusty horse crests the hill. Before you is a vast expanse of territory. You don't know if there's danger out there. So you look around. A copse of trees to the left ... a lake in the distance ... a tendril of smoke drifting above a small rise ... a wooden fence close to you on the right with something on it. Your "scan" suggests things look pretty safe.

So you spur your horse to a trot and go to check out that "something" on the fence. It's a piece of paper nailed to a post. You approach. It's a "Wanted Dead or Alive" poster. You dismount and get a bit closer, and "skim" the contents, looking first for the most salient facts that will help you decide if you need to bother with the fine print. Maybe you've seen the guy. Maybe it's you!

See the difference between scanning and skimming? Now let's apply it to your Web site.

Your visitor arrives and her eyes immediately begin scoping out the situation to determine if she's in the right place. First, she will scan the visible screen for prominent elements, determining if they mesh with her mental image of her mission. As she scans, in addition to collecting "top-level" clues like headlines, she will be evaluating larger-scale issues such as legibility, arrangement and accessibility. This is where the more prominent features including the size of your type, the layout of your page and your use of color come into play. You want to help her minimize the time she spends on finding, sorting, and selecting information and get her engaged in the conversion process. If she doesn't find top-level clues that she's in the right place, or if she finds the page too hard to deal with, she's back on her horse, galloping to another site.

Skimming is the second - but no less important - activity. It is a reading-based activity, a refinement in the information-gathering process. When your visitor has a fairly good idea of the lay of the land, she is going to start engaging with your copy. But she's not ready to stop and read anything thoroughly. She's still not sure whether it will be worth her while. So she's going to start with just a superficial read, looking for the highlights and the important key words that will help direct further involvement. This is where bolding key words, bulleting, keeping paragraphs short, making sure the first and last sentences in each paragraph are strong, choosing a legible font, and even the effective use of hyperlinks all make a difference.

It's a subtle distinction, but one that can make a big difference in your results. Try it - you'll like it!

Point of Action: Location Matters

You don't really need us to tell you that when people visit your site, you need them to realize right away both the value of your product or service and the value of buying from you over one of your competitors. That's pretty basic information.

But think about what's implicit in that information. Right when your visitor lands on the site, he has to get the impression he's in the right place to accomplish the task he has in mind. The information you provide is critical to the impression.

The same is true for every place on your site where you ask your visitors to take action. When you provide your reassuring policies on privacy, returns, guarantees, shipping and so forth (and you do offer these, right?), put them at the Point of Action.

If you want to subscribe to GrokDotCom, you've got to share a little information - not tons of it, just your name and e-mail. But some people are understandably squeamish about doing even that, so we've got a privacy policy. You can scroll all the way down to the bottom of our page and read: "We will never give, lease or sell your personal information. Period!"

Thing is, while that policy is clear, concise and compelling, it's at the bottom of the page. The opt-in subscription box is at the top. You might never get to the bottom to read how sincerely concerned we are about your privacy. So what did we do? We put a concise little statement right under the Subscribe Now button, right at the point of action: "We Value Your Privacy!"

Want to know something? As soon as we did that seemingly minor thing, subscriptions went way up! By putting the information at the point of action, the impact was immediate and dramatic.

Think about how often information that's critical to your customer gets buried in tiny type at the bottom of the page or in some other place where it is not immediately visible when the need to know it is foremost in your visitor's mind.

If you walk into a store, it's fairly easy to find out product warranty information. You can read the box or chat with a salesperson. Online, give your customers this same option, at the point of action, when they'd figuratively be examining that box. Link right there to product warranties, your company's specific policies, even optional extended service plans. Right there! Maybe you take them to the info, maybe you give it to them in a pop-up (about the only time we like these things), maybe you give them a short and sweet sentence.

Getting the picture?

At the exact point your visitor has to start filling in a form with personal information, let her know her privacy is sacred to you.

At the point she might be curious about your company's shipping costs, make them concretely available.

Just when she's wondering whether or not she can return the item if it doesn't suit her, make sure she knows you have a no-questions-asked return policy.

And don't limit yourself to policies. Some shoppers value what other people had to say about a product or about doing business with you. Offer testimonials, but also be sure to put them where they need to be seen, when the question is in your prospect's mind. Think about other aspects of your sales process. What else does your visitor want to know, and when will it have the most impact on his or her decision? It's not only about making sure it's on your site, it's also about making sure it's in the location that will have the most positive impact on your sales.

Think Point of Action. Give them *what* they need to know *when* and *where* they need to know it. Your customers will be delighted that you've managed to anticipate their needs, and that goes a very long way to persuading them you're the folks with whom they want to do business.

What You Need to Know about Writing for Search Engines

Search engines are all about relevance. So the writing you do that is targeted for search engine optimization also needs to be about relevance.

Ever notice when you use a search engine, you are extremely task-oriented? You are only interested in finding the most relevant result that pertains to your search. Then you want to move on. You initiate a search, get a list of choices that potentially meet your need and find the one you want - the end result is that you have been satisfied.

It's analogous to shopping on a Web site. Remember the buying process? Your prospects begin with a problem, they then do an information search, evaluate alternatives and finally decide on the best one to meet their need.

This process also ties in very well with the process of Attention, Interest, Desire, Action and Satisfaction (AIDAS).

Search engines practice both these processes on a regular basis.

Your attention starts after you enter your keywords and keyphrases. You get a ranking of results, the titles of each result capture your interest, the descriptions ignite your desire. Hopefully once you take action and click, you will be satisfied with your choice. If you're not, you'll go through the process once more.

So how can we take the success of the search engines and magnify the effect so that we can increase the conversion rates on our site? Take advantage of the same elements that make your page relevant to the search engines - they just so happen to be the same elements that make the page relevant (and persuasive) to your prospects.

You begin by finding the right keywords and keyphrases.

Researching Keywords and Keyphrases:

There are now a number of resources to assist you in identifying the most popular of relevant keywords. A useful tool provided by Overture, called the "Search Term Suggestion Tool",[40] tells you how many times users searched on a particular key word or phrase in their search engine during the last month. This helps you determine the relative popularity of keywords, which will help you choose the words to include for the search engine spiders.

Additional keyword brainstorming tools worth investigating include WordTracker,[41] Google's terrific Adword Select Keyword Suggestion tool,[42] and customer discussion sites like ePinions and PlanetFeedback.

Stick primarily to two to four word phrases rather than individual words. Because of the staggering number of web pages that are indexed by the major search engines, competing for a spot on the first or second page of search results on a one-word keyword will be a tough battle to win. You'll just be one of thousands of web sites vying for that top position.

Another reason to focus on phrases is that Internet users learn over time to refine their searches in order to get more relevant results. Someone searching for "email marketing glossary" instead of "email marketing" will get a fraction of search results, and those results will be much more useful to them.

The good news is that achieving a top ten position for a search phrase such as "email marketing glossary" is a much more attainable goal and will yield a much more qualified prospect. Also, be aware that there may be times when one spelling variation (like email marketing) pulls better than another variation (e-mail marketing). However, do not use two different spelling variations on the same page; it looks like a typo and breaks your reader's flow.

Some additional tips for keyword research:

+ Include several permutations of the phrases (different order).
+ Create phrases that are in the form of a question.
+ Include synonyms and substitutes to selected words.
+ Include common misspellings.

[40] http://inventory.overture.com/d/searchinventory/suggestion/.
[41] http://www.wordtracker.com/.
[42] https://adwords.google.com/select/main?cmd=KeywordSandbox

- Include brand names of merchandise carried (be sure you stock it).
- Include model numbers of the products you carry.
- Mine the data from a site's internal search engine to see how people found you and what they are looking for on your site (search log data).

Areas to Place Your Keywords and Keyphrases:

- Title tags
- Headings and subheadings (using heading tags <h1>,<h2>,etc.)
- Body text (the most important area, search engines love content, and so do your prospects, make sure the phrase shows up in your first paragraph)
- Link text and navigation
- Meta-tags (keywords and descriptions)
- Alt-attribute in the image source tags

The key is getting your keywords and keyphrases in these areas. It is important to spend plenty of time researching these keywords and making sure they are the terms your visitors use. Remember, "talk to the dog, in the language of the dog about what is in the heart of the dog."

Don't worry if you aren't technically literate; just understand that you want to be in control of the content that goes in those important areas.

Beyond Search Engine Positioning

It's tough to convert traffic if you don't have any, know what we mean? You probably know search engines remain the most popular way people find websites and account for over 80% of the traffic to some sites.

Having a website that's a killer conversion machine is a big part of improving your results. So is insuring a high ranking in search engine positioning. But beyond positioning, you want to make sure what the search retrieves is persuasive and drives action.

What good's a high ranking that's so badly worded, nobody clicks on it? Or an okay-worded ranking that brings in only a fraction of the traffic you'd get if your copy captured browsers' attention and moved them to action? Not good ... in fact, maybe even doubly bad! You look undependable if your listing is so terse it seems like you can't be bothered with the details.

Worse, suppose you sit at the top of the list with a vague, misleading blurb. Imagine how annoyed folks are going to be when they click through and don't find what they expected. And guess what happens when you lure folks to a site that fails to deliver and doesn't engage them in the conversion process?

Conversion is about getting prospects to take the action you want them to take. For search engines, the action you want to motivate is a click. Here's what you need to know so you get the clicks you want.

An SEOP Fable

Phil sells designer clothes for pet sharks. He goes to a Search Engine Optimization (SEOP) company to generate traffic for his niche market. The company says it will do several things: identify valuable keywords, get him high rankings on top search engines, optimize his home page and create an information page (an added webpage that is keyword rich). Phil checks the company out and gives their proposal a thumb's up.

They get busy and locate some keywords and synonyms, then proceed to optimize Phil's home page, targeting the phrase "Shark Clothes." Since the SEOP expert's goal is a high ranking, she puts "Shark Clothes" in the title tag of the home page (part of the HTML code the search engine looks for). She succeeds! Phil gets a top ranking on Google that looks like this:

Shark Clothes

... for sharks who are fashion-conscious and shark owners who are embarrassed by their naked pets.

Like most SEOP companies, this one is good at getting high rankings, but it doesn't understand conversion. What we have here is a top ranking that doesn't drive action. No persuasion. No calls to action. No real appeal to benefits. The conversion rate of this ranking will be a fraction of what's possible.

Compare that listing with this one:

Buy Top Designer Shark Clothes Now and Get FREE Shipping

Are you a hip shark looking to stand out from the school? A shark owner who wants to strut your pet in finery on his morning walk? Phil has what you need.

What's different? The imperative "Buy" gets attention and creates momentum toward taking action. "Now" reinforces the urgency. FREE shipping provides a clear benefit. Then a "richer" descriptive sentence appeals to emotion and creates strong mental imagery. This listing is likely to get 20-50% more clicks than the first one!

And all we did was add a few very important words in a very specific way to create a link that doesn't just sit there, but actively converts traffic.

In Conclusion

The Grok Notes

Cliff Notes are cool, aren't they? When you want to cut to the chase, you buy one and it reveals exactly what you were supposed to get out of, say, *Moby Dick*. Saves you a lot of life energy if you are the sort who isn't into plowing through the original, but wants a clear understanding of the salient points.

Know your audience

Elena Fawkner discovered this snippet of copy from the Web site of a professional Web copywriter:

> Today's readers and Web browsers demand frankness and verisimilitude, so your written communications require exacting professional integrity with accurate and adequate research. For concrete, colorful and dynamic written material that willfully attracts customers, Bob Tony* will work with you to develop unrivaled written communications for your marketing materials, grants, newsletters, Web site, or other publications and articles. To ensure your writing tasks with pacesetting presentation and unparalleled, consistent editorial power, give your deadlines to Bob Tony*.
>
> * Name changed to protect the ostentatious and largiloquent.[43]

Verisimilitude? Willfully attracts? Ensure with pacesetting presentation? Editorial power? What a mouth- and headful of gobbledygook! Bob Tony is definitely not the fellow you want as your copywriting model!

---

[43] "Writing for the Web." Elena Fawkner. Internet Day, 14 December 2001.

Where do you look? To your customers! Folks are out there talking. So listen to what they have to say and how they say it, then model your copy to reflect their needs and concerns. If you're going to invest time doing "adequate research," dig in here!

Keep your copy customer-centered

Ditch self-serving copy that promotes how wonderful you are. Focus on the powerful perspective of the second person (YOU!) to help your visitors put themselves inside the picture, and always let your visitors know what's in it for them by communicating the benefits of your product or service. Appeal to their emotions by showing rather than telling and by engaging the senses.

Create a personality

For all its interactivity and dynamism, the Web isn't very personal. And you want to get as nose-to-nose with folks as you can. Do it not only by writing as you (and they) would speak, but also by creating the impression of an appealing personality. Give your writing a distinctive, memorable style that captivates as it persuades. And keep in mind: who you are is far less important than who your visitors imagine you to be.

VERBal power

Verbs get your visitors excited and should form the backbone of your writing.

Using active verbs will not only help keep your visitors engaged, it will also help improve your credibility. The passive voice occasionally may help you set the right tone or focus on the activity rather than the actor, but for persuasive purposes, it tends to sound shifty and overly academic. In general, avoid it in your Web copy.

Imperative verbs are commands. Act. Drive. Click. See. Go. Download. Pair them with benefits and you have effective calls to action.

Be credible

Your copy sends out credibility vibes all the time. Over-promising and spouting lots of marketing hype won't work in your favor. Neither will typos and grammatical errors.

Make your copy usability-friendly

Understanding human eye-tracking behavior helps you optimize the organization of your copy on your Web pages. It also helps to understand how folks scan and skim copy.

- Use bulleted points to detail critical information (including your value proposition)
- Get important information to your visitor first; elaborate later (think newspaper articles)
- Highlight important text by using bolding, color, a highlight feature, or making the critical text a link (as appropriate)
- Use "white" space to separate your points
- Keep your paragraphs concise and small -eyes glaze over when they encounter impenetrable blocks of text
- Use font sizes that don't require magnifying glasses
- Avoid light type against a dark background (reverse type) - stick with contrast combinations that are comfortable on the eye

Is that everything? Sheesh, you know me well enough by now to know that when it comes to your online copy, I could keep going till the cows come home. But then, these wouldn't be The Grok Notes, would they? And you wouldn't know which areas I think are most important to your efforts.

Now you do!

What to Do Next

It can be daunting to consider revamping the entirety of the copy on your Web site. And it isn't necessarily something we would recommend you do all at once.

If you have an existing site, you are in the advantageous position of being able to test and optimize your changes. So as you are making improvements, you are also learning much more intimately the strategies and tactics that work best in your situation, for your audience. Tiny, incremental changes will yield far more valuable information than a sweeping overhaul.

As you begin to make those changes, we offer these suggestions:

1. Don't feel overwhelmed with the task before you. It may seem large, but breaking it into bite-sized chunks is a much better - and saner - approach.

2. Look to the "low-hanging fruit" first. There are many opportunities to change obvious, simple elements of your copy that can have a dramatic effect on your conversion rate. Here are some possibilities:

    a. Start paying close attention to your Web logs.[44] For now, look carefully at your reject pages - the ones where visitors exit or fail to take an action. Determine the extent to which the page is critical to the buying process, then evaluate the copy to see if you can make improvements that will keep your visitors motivated and moving.

---

[44] For more information on conversion metrics, refer to Measuring, Testing and Optimizing on page 154.

b. Examine all the areas on your site where you require or request your visitor to supply personal information. Add point of action statements that assure your visitor's need to feel secure. We added the very brief "We value your privacy" beneath the newsletter subscribe button for a client and subscription rates immediately doubled!

c. On key Web pages, examine your headings (these are the words that grab attention) and your benefits (these are the points that build interest). Make sure your headings are written in language that is benefit-oriented. Bullet your benefits so visitors can quickly read them, and make sure they address what "matters to the hearts of your dogs." We made changes to fewer than 40 words in the headings and benefit copy for one client who was experiencing a high rejection rate on one page. After the changes, hundreds more visitors completed that page and moved forward in the conversion process.

d. Scrutinize your autoresponder messaging and your emails. In the messages you send to your customers - from shipping confirmations to promotional offers - you have a wonderful opportunity to stretch your writing wings and nurture a (hopefully) long-term relationship.

3. With every change you make, always test and optimize. Even if they all seem necessary, changes need to be made individually so you can track the result of the change. If you make one change at a time and then discover it doesn't help, it's easier to back up and try something else. If you are not methodical in your approach to change, much of your effort will be wasted.

4. Learn one skill at a time, and understand it in the context of your particular situation. Your goal is not to follow e-commerce rules (they don't exist, anyway); your goal is to understand the principles of conversion and how they apply to you. What works like a dream for one Web site is not necessarily going to work in the same way for another. We've examined many of the principles that relate to

relevant writing for the Web. Your circumstance will dictate how those principles apply. There is no fast-track to certain success - remember the Tortoise! So take your time. Be methodical. In the long run, it will be worth it.

This is exciting stuff, and it's just about to get more exciting! We wish you all the best.

Understanding
Online Conversion

Introduction

You have goals for your visitors - you want them to make purchases, subscribe, register, make referrals, enter contests, qualify as leads, and so forth. Your visitors have goals, too. They come to you - through search engines, email, surfing, recommendations - in the hope they will find something to add value to their lives and/or businesses. They look to you to help them fulfill their needs, as well as provide a process that not only satisfies, but delights.

Conversion is the complex, multi-faceted process whereby your Web site and emails persuade your visitors to take the action you want them to take. Your Conversion Rate is a measure of your ability to persuade your visitors to take that action. It is a reflection both of your effectiveness and your customers' satisfaction.

Understanding the rationale behind everything that goes into creating effective Web presence that drives action and builds relationships is essential - it gives you the framework for acknowledging the value and the role of all the components. Knowing why you need to do something in a particular way strengthens your ability to create successful customer experiences.

Your short-term goal is to persuade those who visit your website or get your email to read it and take action on it. Your long-term goal is to develop ongoing relationships with your prospects, so when they think of the products and services you offer, they will turn - and return - to you. How you accomplish this is only peripherally about technology. It is far more about people - who they are, what they feel, what makes them tick, and what they really need from you. And when it comes to communication, it's not what you say, but what they perceive that counts.

The process through which you turn browsers into buyers involves both art and science, and is grounded in proven principles. In this section of the book, we present an overview of these principles and address the steps you need to consider in creating or refining your online conversion process so your visitors will take the steps you desire.

Conversion = Persuasion = "Selling"

Quite simply, whatever you do on your site, whenever there is an exchange of value, wherever you are trying to get your visitors to take an action - any action - you are engaged in selling. More importantly, you are asking your visitors to engage in the process of conversion.

The online world of commerce and content revolves around the simple five-letter word, "sales." Unfortunately, when people hear the word, they think of it as a "dirty" word and imagine a slick, pushy and fast-talking used car salesman. But sales is many things. It can be:

- The exchange of currency for products or services
- The exchange of personal information for entry into a sweepstakes
- Subscribing to a newsletter
- Opting in to an email list
- Registering yourself
- Agreeing to provide a referral
- Converting someone to your opinion about something
- Inspiring someone to get as enthusiastic about something as you are

or even

- Convincing a child she should clean her room
- A child convincing a parent to allow him to stay up 15 minutes longer

In short, sales - a word we use for the sake of simplicity - is all about persuading people to take the action you want them to take. Persuasion is a transactional process resulting in a change in beliefs, attitudes and/or behaviors; it is the mechanism by which you motivate conversion.

You're not going to change anyone's mind; in truth, people don't change their minds. Instead, we reexamine old beliefs and decisions in light of new information that affects how we think or feel, and make decisions based on our reactions to that information. If we ever 'changed' our minds, we simply reconsidered what we knew to be true and how we felt about it. Keep in mind the wisdom of Samuel Butler (1612-1680), who wrote, "He that complies against his will is of his own opinion still." Persuasion is fundamentally a cognitive and emotions-based process.

Conversion is the process whereby visitors to your site become (are "converted" into) customers, subscribers, contest entrants, etc. If conversion is the result of persuasion, then persuasion equals selling, where selling is both the art and science of practicing professional persuasion, using time-tested and proven methods and systems.

Building a Solid Structure

There are three fundamental ways to increase your online revenues:

Increase Traffic. Using this technique, you drive more visitors to your site, on the assumption that more visitors will correlate to an increase in sales. Tactics for increasing traffic, most of which are marketing methods that require you to spend more money, can include advertising, positioning in search engines, public relations campaigns, viral marketing, and encouraging customers to return.

Merchandise. Encouraging your paying customers to spend more money per visit is another way to increase your revenues. You can accomplish this in many ways: cross-selling, up-selling, reevaluating your most effective price points and margins, providing extra services at discount, bundling products or services into "packages," and stressing benefits rather than features. Even something as basic as improving the quality of your copywriting can have a dramatic impact on your results.

Increase Your Conversion Rate. If you concentrate on improving your website's conversion rate (the number of unique visitors who actually buy divided by the total number of unique visitors), you will improve your results without having to spend one more penny to drive more traffic. There are literally thousands of refinements, many of which cost practically nothing to implement, that will increase your results dramatically. A few examples: reduce the number of steps (clicks) in the checkout process, clarify

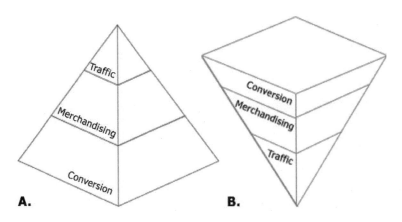

A.   **B.**

your Unique Value Proposition, redesign your navigation scheme and prominently display your privacy assurances and guarantees.

In order to build a stable and profitable online business, you must focus on all these areas. It isn't really a question of what you should include or omit, it's a question of priority and the orderly organization of your efforts. Consider the diagram above.

To build a solid structure, you must first build a site that focuses on maximizing Conversion. Once you have your conversion system in place, you can implement strategies for improving your Merchandising and driving more Traffic. It is the only sane and logical order - the way you can build a business to last like the Great Pyramids of Egypt, rather than one that crumbles under the weight of its own inefficient "design."

The bottom line? To be successful online, you must make conversion your first priority. Only when you have a successful, efficient "machine" that gets the most from your traffic do you have an enterprise in which it makes any sense to invest further precious marketing resources.

The Leaky Bucket

Visitors may arrive on your site interested in what you have to offer, but they still need to be "sold." Propensity to buy is not the same as buying. A Web site that is inefficient at persuading visitors to take the desired action is like an extremely leaky bucket - traffic fills the bucket like water and then leaks out of the holes. It makes sense to plug as many of the holes as possible.

TYPICAL WEBSITE TRAFFIC DROP-OFF

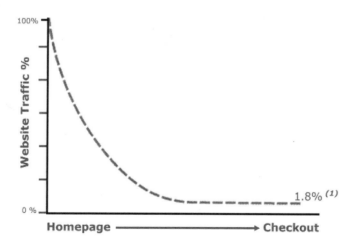

Useful though this metaphor is, it does have limitations: it's impossible to plug all your holes and influence the behaviors of all your visitors. In any sales situation, there is a natural attrition that occurs as people move through the buying process. Sometimes people leave for reasons beyond your control, but more often than not, especially online, they leave for reasons you can control.

Online conversion rates are appallingly low. On average, fewer than two out of every 100 online shoppers actually make a purchase,[1] compared to an offline retail rate of almost 50 percent.[2] Even e-commerce sites with higher conversion rates are only scratching the surface of their potential.

If your drop-off rate is typical, your bucket is very leaky right up front. You're losing a lot more people along the way than you should be losing. The marketing approach to getting more sales in spite of a leaky bucket is to drive more traffic - an expensive and inefficient option that means still more visitors will be subjected to the same leaks. You may experience an overall increase in sales (at considerable cost), but your conversion rate will remain static. And studies prove people who leak out rarely come back, which means the more traffic you drive without fixing the leaks, the more potential customers you lose. Forever.

So focus on methods that increase your conversion rate. You want to get as many people through your sales process as possible, and the most efficient way to make that happen is to engage your visitors in a systematic, professional selling process.

The best way to locate your "leaks" is to turn to your Web logs and evaluate the Single Page Access metric, which will reveal Reject Rates for your home page and key landing pages - instances where visitors arrived on the page, then left, without going further into the Web site. Pages with high Reject Rates indicate that your ability to engage and motivate your visitors is missing the mark. These are pages that require remedial work.

The longer you can keep a visitor fully engaged in the sales process, the less likely that visitor is to bail out. Hence, you want to optimize your efforts to move visitors further into the site. And that means plugging the leaks.

[1] Shop.org.
[2] *Why We Buy*. Paco Underhill. New York: Simon & Schuster. 1999. p 35.

FOR EXAMPLE

One company, Total Gym, specializing in home exercise equipment, had an extremely high rejection rate for its home page, which was essentially a splash page displaying the categories of equipment the company offered. A high rejection rate correlates with a low site penetration rate - visitors are not moving further in the conversion process. When your home page suffers a high rejection rate, it is an indication you are not meeting even the most basic of your visitors' needs. We evaluated where the visitors who did click through went and discovered that nearly 80% went to one category. By simply getting rid of the splash page and establishing the favored category as the home page, we were able to increase Total Gym's conversion rates by almost 40%.

Conversion is Like an Onion

As Shrek might philosophically announce to Donkey, "A conversion system is like an onion." There are layers within the system, each of which must be addressed for the system to work effectively and efficiently.

Conversion takes place and can be measured at many levels in your online efforts. The most obvious level is when your visitor completes a purchase - this is the big picture goal. You have also made a successful conversion when your visitor fills in and submits a form, downloads a file, subscribes, contacts you as a result of exposure to your Web site or email, or even when your visitor simply clicks through to the next step in your process.

Constructing an effective system of conversion requires that you understand the nature of the actions you are motivating. If you consider conversion simply a function of the end result, you will miss the boat.

- Actions are taken only after making a decision.
- Your visitors' goals are "macro-actions."
- Every macro-action is composed of a series of smaller "micro-actions."

The graphic on the opposite page depicts a conversion funnel - the step-by-step process typical of many commerce Web sites. To move from step to step, your visitor takes part in a series of decisions that result in micro-conversions, and at any point along the way, your visitor may decide (or be persuaded) to abandon the effort. At each step of the sales process, you lose people. We spoke of this "drop off" and used a "leaky bucket" metaphor to describe the inability of your process to successfully convert all your visitors or prospects.

Unfortunately, most people measure conversion by the complete macro-action they want prospects to take (e.g., how many people made a purchase, subscribed, registered, etc). Yet every one of these actions is composed of a series of smaller actions. Each micro-action, or omission thereof, is a potential hole in your bucket, a place where you risk losing someone.

Take Microsoft, for instance. Microsoft wanted to get people to download Internet Explorer 6 - the macro-action. When they first released Internet Explorer 6, the top image in the center column of the Internet Explorer home page had the following text: "Download Internet Explorer 6 now. Experience the latest in private, reliable and flexible Internet browsing." The ultimate goal is to get Jane Consumer to download and install the browser on her PC.

But here's an outline of all the necessary micro-actions Jane must take to accomplish the macro-action:

1. She finds the link for IE 6 on the home page
2. She understands it
3. She clicks on it
4. From the main Internet Explorer page she can choose to:
   a. download immediately
   b. order a CD
   c. learn more

5. If she chooses to learn more, the goal still is to get her back on track to download or order a CD
6. If she then chooses to download IE 6:
    a.   Her first action is to select which language she wants
    b.   Then she must click on the link to start downloading the setup file
7. If instead she chooses to order a CD:
    a.   She must decide which CD she wants to order (there are two options)
    b.   Once the action of choosing the CD is complete, she is taken to step one of the form
    c.   There, she must fill out the form
    d.   Then she must click to submit the form

This constitutes a lot of micro-actions - lots of opportunities for leaks. To plug the holes in the leaky bucket, you need to measure and evaluate the drop-off activity for every step - through analyzing your Web logs, you essentially follow the navigation path your visitor takes. Where your visitor leaves, or where she appears to have redirected her involvement, you zoom in with a magnifying glass.

Your conversion system should always be focusing on getting the visitor to take an action - even if that action is simply to move on to the next step in the process. So, whenever you are constructing a system of conversion, these are the questions to keep in mind:

- Has the sales path clearly mapped the actions your prospects should take?
- How well are prospects guided step-by-step?
- How many leaks are left?
- How many prospects are falling through them?

As you are working at the micro-level, you need to answer these three questions:

- What actions satisfy all your objectives?
- Who needs to be persuaded to take action?
- How do you persuade them most effectively to take action?

Sales is a Five-Step Process

Would you build a great store, stock it with great products, run ads to drive traffic to your store, but not hire any salespeople? Would you expect your customers to feel comfortable choosing products and buying them on their own? If your Web site doesn't employ active selling techniques, that's what's happening - in which case, the best you can do is hope your customers will buy.

Can you afford that?

It doesn't matter what you "sell" - whether it's stuff, a service, entertainment, a cause, or information, online and offline, B2C or B2B - the sales process is the same. If you want your Web site to sell more, you have to construct it so it employs the five-step selling process. This is how you create an intentional rather than an accidental system of conversion.

The five steps of the sales process are: Prospect, Rapport, Qualify, Present, and Close. Notice the process isn't strictly linear. Rapport, Qualify and Present are iterative; each step feeds and influences the others as the overall process moves toward the close (assuming you do it correctly). Any good salesperson knows selling is a process of evaluation and reevaluation - for both the salesperson and the prospective customer.

The Prospect step is usually where Marketing does its thing - delivering lots of qualified traffic (people interested in what you have to offer). You pique your potential customers' interests, and once you've brought them to your site, the very first thing you do is reinforce their feeling that they are in the right place by presenting your Unique Value Proposition (UVP).

Your UVP isn't a slogan or phrase designed for your advertising, although that's one potential use for it. Rather, it is the concise and memorable statement that powerfully describes the unique value of your business and creates excitement in the visitor. Its purpose is to answer the question always implicit in your visitors' minds: "Why should I do business with you and not somebody else?"

Drop-off rates are frequently due to a Web site's inability to present a credible answer to this question, certainly on the home page, but also on critical landing pages. The key metric that generally helps you identify where you need to strengthen your customer-centered value propositions is the Single Page Access Report.

Once your qualified visitors arrive, your site must immediately begin the process of building Rapport. Lacking the face-to-face, and often non-verbal, elements of communication available to us in the offline world, you develop rapport online in many other ways:

- Through the speed of your download
- Through the appearance of your site
- Through design elements that promote trust
- Through content elements that promote trust
- Through ease of navigation
- Through the power of your copy
- Through the relevance of your images
- Through exceptional customer service
- Through assurances and privacy policies

You make no assumptions about your visitors' prior knowledge, either about computer literacy or the nature of your products or services. You offer clear access to help and provide relevant information. You also acknowledge that people have different personality types that influence how they shop. You use your understanding of personality types to adapt your sales process to the individual, so you sell to people in the way they want to be sold to. People do want to be sold and need to be guided by an expert (you); they just don't want to be pushed.

Qualifying is key to eventually closing the sale. After all, is there any reason why you wouldn't buy if you were shown exactly what you wanted? So you must qualify skillfully. This is where your site must help visitors identify the best product or service for their needs. Yet discovering exactly what your visitors want is your biggest challenge.

In the bricks-and-mortar world, you would begin a dialog. Online, since you can't "ask" the questions, you make them implicit in the hyperlinks you offer. There are four types of visitors:

1. Those who know exactly want they want
2. Those who know approximately what they want
3. Those who don't know what they want, but if they found it, they would buy it
4. Those who got there by accident and don't want anything

You need navigation and information architecture that address each possibility.

As you work through the process of Qualifying, you Present, offering products or services that are the right "answers" to your visitors' "questions." And, although it might seem "early" in the process, you also must begin to Close the sale. Closing involves answering your visitors' concerns about doing business with you, resolving objections, encouraging completion of the exchange of value, detailing service plans, offering payment options, and explaining your guarantees.

These critical assurances cannot be placed randomly throughout your Web site, but must appear specifically at the Point of Action (POA), where it matters most to your visitors. These assurances inspire trust and confidence, and make a huge difference to your visitors' decision to Close.

Whether you are creating a single email or an entire Web site, you must acknowledge every step of this process. Remember, too, there are feedback loops in the overall trajectory - so it's not unusual to have two, three, or even all five steps operating on a single Web page.

Think of the sales process as working on both a micro-level and a macro-level at the same time: the micro-level is the individual page or the specific task visitors are focused on; the macro-level is the entire online experience - from the time visitors arrive on your site up to and through the close, and even beyond, to your after-sales service and support.

FOR EXAMPLE

We cannot over-emphasize the power of POA as an effective component of your conversion efforts. One client's objectives included increasing the number of subscribers to his newsletter. To subscribe, a visitor needed only supply a first and last name, and an email address - not an enormous amount of personal information, but enough to make many people understandably nervous. We placed the graphic call to action in the top right corner of his home page (a particularly effective location), and right below the subscribe button added four words: "We Value Your Privacy!" Immediately, the conversion rate for subscriptions on our client's site doubled.

The Sales Process in Action Online

Our inimitable friend, The Grok,[3] explains how the five-step selling process translates from the real world to both a Web site and an email promoting a direct transaction.

Prospecting

Let's say you are trying to sell bicycles. You run ads featuring this magnificent new trail bike that's hit the market. You've whetted people's appetites, and they start coming into your store to see this cool bike. So what's the first thing you want them to see when they walk in? Well, it ain't the helmet and water-bottle rack!

> **Apply this to your Web site**: If you've marketed that cool bike, you'd better spotlight it prominently on the very first page your customer sees. Of course you sell lots of other bikes and accessories, and you can include information about or link to those as well. But if you drive customers to you for a specific reason and then don't deliver immediately, you've lost them.

> **Apply this to your email**: If you've announced a particular item to your prospects and persuaded them to click through, you'd better be sending them to the landing page that features that item. No, not the home page or even a sub-category page. Take them to *the item*. Yes, absolutely, that landing page can and should suggest

[3] The Grok, Future Now's Martian mascot, is a keen observer of the world around him and takes a particular interest in the World Wide Web. He discourses on conversion-related matters through Future Now's newsletter, GrokDotCom. "Grok, "a Martian word that implies the presence of intimate and exhaustive knowledge and understanding, is taken from the landmark novel *Stranger in a Strange Land*, by Robert A. Heinlein.

there's a world of wealth beyond. But you've made an offer and an implicit promise. Fulfill it directly. If they found the email relevant, your site must reinforce the relevance.

Rapport

As soon as a customer enters your store, you don't ignore them, do you? You begin to develop Rapport. The process actually starts with the appearance of your store and the arrangement of products, and then is augmented by the availability of help, the knowledgeability of sales staff and the personable way customers are treated. Everything a customer experiences in your store feeds into that sense of rapport. Naturally, you want it all to reflect well on you. You want your customer to feel confident about buying.

> **Apply this to your Web site**: When you're online, you lack that N2N (nose-to-nose) element, so you develop rapport through the speed of your download, the professional appearance of your site, through elements that promote trust, through ease of navigation, through the power of your text and the relevance of your images, and through exceptional customer service. You treat your online visitors intelligently, but make no assumptions about their prior knowledge, either computer- or product-related. You offer clear access to help and provide concise, relevant information. You also understand there are different basic personalities, and everyone has a particular way in which they prefer to be sold.

> **Apply this to your email**: What goes for the Web site goes for your email, with one elaboration: the appearance of your communication on the preview screen says a lot about you in those first crucial moments. This is where image is going to count for a lot (with the glorious substance to follow). Copy should engage and make a connection with the reader. Instructions must be clear and easy to follow. Folks are going to invest less time with an email than they might on your Web site. After all, how many emails do they get a day ... and how long do you think they linger over a communication that doesn't speak to them immediately?

Qualifying and Presenting

Now, let's suppose a woman walks into your store and looks a bit out of place. You go up to her and ask if you can help. "I'm looking for a bike." (Aha, you think, she's come to the right place ... bikes I got!) You don't know, however, what sort of bike she wants. Maybe she doesn't even know this herself. Maybe all she wants to do is browse and needs the tiniest nudge from you in any direction. Or maybe she has a general idea and needs specific information. So you begin a dialog with her. You ask questions to identify and Qualify just what she wants. Browsing? Here's the general layout of our store. Trekking bikes? Over there. Touring bikes? On that far wall. You want a child's bike? You'll find a great selection right here.

As you gradually get a better idea of her needs, you Present certain options to her. You show her a handsome silver and blue child's bike with training wheels. She tells you her son is ten and stands about so tall. You show her a different bike. Qualifying and presenting are iterative; you go back and forth until you've narrowed the field to *the* bike.

> **Apply this to your Web site**: Think of this as the iterative process that helps your customer identify the best product to meet her needs. Since you can't "ask" the questions, you must provide the options, making it very clear that in the category of kids' bikes, you offer tricycles, bikes with training wheels, bikes for mid-sized kids, bikes that will appeal to girls, bikes that will appeal to boys, bikes for different purposes, bikes in different price ranges. What you do not do is waste your online customer's precious time (any more than you would in a real world store) by showing her something she isn't interested in buying. But you need to do more than just present the most relevant information. You need to keep your prospect moving ahead in the process of ultimately deciding to buy, and you do that by applying the concept of AIDAS: getting her Attention, strengthening her Interest, stimulating her Desire (even if only for more information), motivating her to take Action (even if it's just clicking to drill deeper), and then making 200% sure you Satisfy her with the result.[4]

---

[4] For more information on AIDAS, refer to pages 136-138.

Apply this to your email: By themselves, emails are not very interactive. You send, they read, maybe they click through. Moreover, the ostensible purpose of the email might not be a direct sale - perhaps you are presenting information, or offering seasonal wishes, focusing more on the relationship than immediate action. (In these situations, the purpose of your email is to reinforce rapport, and overtly including other aspects of the sales process may work against you.) Certainly you can develop a degree of qualifying and presenting (Lands End does this exceptionally well in their mailings offering selected items in multiple categories). Ultimately, your email is one step in the cycle of qualifying and presenting: it should encourage your reader to click through to a landing page, where your Web site can offer a more interactive experience of this phase.

Closing

You've done a great job so far. The woman seems inclined to buy her son the blue Wheelie you showed her, but she has several questions, perhaps even some objections. Here is where you must begin to Close the sale. You answer her questions, resolve her objections, encourage the close, detail your available service plans, offer payment options and explain your guarantees. You communicate that you stand behind your products. You provide security and confidence, a sense she will not be forgotten the second she leaves with that blue bike.

> **Apply this to your Web site**: Post your privacy policies (and honor them scrupulously), post your guarantees, offer every ordering option you can (online, fax, phone), prominently display a toll-free customer service telephone number (and staff it with a well-trained person, please!), make checking out clear and painless - even inviting - don't ask for unnecessary information, offer an opportunity for customer feedback, provide shipping and delivery details, don't hide any charges, confirm the sale. And more. AIDAS helps you here, too. If you've set up your buy funnel correctly and done everything right, buying will be your customer's natural next step, but you still have to close, or an awful lot of sales will slip right through your digital fingers. Plus, you

gotta remember the sales process is never concluded when the customer leaves. Your most profitable business is repeat business. Let your customers know you appreciate them, and give them reasons to come back.

Apply this to your email: As on your Web site, your email needs to contain important assurances that include your commitment to privacy, your guarantees, a telephone contact, even the knowledge that prospects can opt-out if they absolutely don't want to hear another word from you. Folks won't be "checking out," adding items to shopping carts or filling out forms directly on your email - in this respect, your email is one step on your reader's journey - but sensitivity to Closing issues is important.

By applying these steps, you engage your shoppers not only in the physical dimension of colors, shapes, sizes, and prices, but you also appeal to the critical emotional and psychological dimensions that underlie every decision to buy. You may not be N2N with your online customers, but you can make them feel as though you are. They want this, they respond well to this. Moreover, they expect it.

Buying is the Flip Side of Selling

Online sales would be easy if it were merely a matter of driving traffic to your site and presenting your product or service. But e-businesses have discovered the equation is not so simple. One of the primary reasons this simplistic offering routinely fails is because people, whether they are aware of it or not, go through a complex mental process before, during, and after a purchase.

When it comes to how people make the decision to buy, there is one important axiom:

People rationalize buying decisions based on facts,
but
People MAKE buying decisions based on feelings.

Emotions inform every decision we make. A University of Rochester School of Medicine study that employed brain activity imaging revealed emotions are an inextricable part of the decision process. In fact, "if you eliminate the emotional guiding factors, it's impossible [for people] to make decisions in daily life."[5] People with damaged prefrontal lobes - the area of the brain where emotions are processed - are completely stymied when it comes to making personal decisions such as scheduling a doctor's appointment, wearing a seat belt, even deciding what to buy for themselves! When humans make personal decisions, they put themselves in the picture and evaluate the emotional risks or gains of making that decision. If they can't grasp an emotional image, they can't make the decision.

[5] "Getting Emotional is a Rational Decision." Lee Bowman, Brain Connection. http://www.brainconnection.com.

To successfully get your visitors to take action you must be able to see the world from their "buying" point of view. Ideally, while maintaining your sales perspective, you conduct your sales process so it is in tune with how people make these decisions.

Whenever people make a buying decision, that decision represents the culmination of a process. It may take place almost instantaneously or stretch out over a long period of time - but it's a process, not an event. For this reason, it is important to consider that not all visitors are prepared or even inclined to make a decision when they first visit your site - sometimes a successful conversion is the result of multiple visits.

No matter how long the process takes, the buying decision always begins when people become aware of a need. Once they have identified that need, they begin to search for and explore possible avenues for meeting it. While gathering information, they refine and evaluate all the buying criteria that will affect the decision to purchase and narrow the field of choice to the "best few" alternatives. Once they reach a decision and choose, they take action by making a purchase. It's important to keep in mind, as shopping cart abandonment rates indicate, making a decision to purchase is not the same thing as completing the purchase. The final step in the process involves a reevaluation of the decision and its results.

To summarize, the steps of the buying decision process are:

- Identify
- Search
- Evaluate
- Decide
- Purchase
- Reevaluate

The way people make buying decisions depends on the complexity of the problem they are trying to solve and the complexity of each step in the decision process. This will affect how you manage the sale:

- If their needs and the decision-making process are simple, all you need to do is make your visitors aware of you, build confidence, differentiate yourself, demonstrate value and guide them through a very simple shopping and buying process. This is why lower-end, branded products sell so well. Think of buying a book from Amazon.com.

- If their needs and the decision-making process are highly complex, then you need to approach the sale slightly differently. This type of sale requires you to make people aware of you, build relationships, educate them (and perhaps many different individuals or teams within the same organization), show sensitivity to the different decision-makers, influencers and groups, and resolve conflicting needs, so you can custom-tailor your solutions and make the buying process as painless and positive as possible. Think of purchasing a multi-million dollar piece of equipment that needs five departments to sign off to close the deal.

Analyzing your Web logs for individual navigation activity paths, beyond helping you determine which pages inspire your visitors to leave, will allow you to gather critical information on how your visitors use your site with respect to the buying decision process.

When customers become aware of a need, they need to know you offer a solution. Only when they know you provide value that matters to them can you undertake building the foundations of a satisfying relationship by establishing rapport and trust. To accomplish this, you must not only "speak" to their "felt" needs, you must speak in ways that appeal to the emotions and ignite powerful, evocative mental imagery in your prospects' minds - the sort of imagery that allows them to put themselves center stage. You must be able to offer your prospects the emotional dimensions of meaning and value that help them decide.

FOR EXAMPLE

Max-Effect, a yellow-page advertising design company, was experiencing a problem with product presentation. Ideally, the company wanted to see visitors land on the home page, go to view product samples, then click through to contact and pricing information. But many of the visitors who made it past the home page were leaving on the samples page.

We examined the page and found a collection of 13 advertisements the company had designed presented artfully on a black background. The ads were exceptional, but because yellow-page advertising is basically non-distinct enough that it begs forgetting, visitors didn't quite realize how impressed they should be.

We scrapped the artful collection and opted to present Max-Effect's work in a before-and-after format more sensitive to the buying decision process, pairing the ad Max-Effect designed to the one the client formerly had run in the yellow pages.

The change helped work conversion wonders - Max-Effect went from 5-7 leads a month to 2-3 leads a week!

Yellow Page
Ad Samples

Some Yellow Page Ads Generate a Phenomenal Response.
Now YOURS Can Too!

Click thumbnails for larger image.

Before MaxEffect   **After MaxEffect**

Tuning in to WIIFM

You will never increase your conversion rate by pushing what you want to sell in the way you want to sell it; rather, you need to construct the type of environment that naturally leads your customers through buying the way they want to buy. Your ultimate goal is to delight each of your visitors, for the delighted customer is the one most likely to complete a purchase, refer your business to others and return to buy again.

At the most fundamental level, we all are motivated by a single, critical question: What's in it for me (we call it everyone's favorite radio station, WIIFM)? Our dominant personality types strongly influence how we ask that question, perceive value and, consciously or, more typically, subconsciously, approach decision-making.

We present an overview of the four dominant personality types in "Writing for Personalities."[6] Rather than repeat that information here, we would like to emphasize how important it is to acknowledge each personality type through all your online efforts.

Imagine you - an impressionistic, Expressive type - go to a bricks-and-mortar store to purchase a digital camera. All you want is a camera that takes pictures and isn't a big hassle, so you can have a good time. The salesperson comes on like a know-it-all and rattles on about pixels and resolutions and cabling and any number of other technical considerations you really could care less about. You want to know, and truly only care, whether the camera is going to fit into your lifestyle. Will it be a good match for your expectations and how you generally use techie gadgets like this? If the salesperson can't communicate the information you need to know, in the way you want to learn it, you're not going to be happy. You

---

[6] Refer to pages 72-76.

are going to start tuning out the salesperson. And you'll probably walk away none-the-wiser, as well as cameraless.

Now, imagine you are a very Analytic sort of person. You've done the research; you understand all the ramifications of a digital camera's features and inherently understand the advantages or disadvantages of each feature. To feel comfortable about a purchase, you need to know you are getting a camera designed to meet your criteria. You want to speak with someone who knows all the facts and can answer all your questions. But you get a different salesperson in our theoretical store, and this one wants to tell you all about how easy the camera is to use and shows you print-out images and explains her Mom has one and loves it. This is going to strike you as vague and ditsy. You are going to start tuning out the salesperson and may well conclude she doesn't know the first thing about what she's trying to sell.

Good salespeople know whether or not they are saying what the customer needs to hear, the way the customer needs to hear it, in order to make a decision to purchase. It's one of the most essential components of "the sale."

Acknowledging personality types online is critical - you are conducting business in a self-service medium. You aren't there to modify your persuasion tactics when you notice they aren't working. You only notice they haven't worked when you check out your Web logs. Online it's the responsibility of your hyperlinks to establish, maintain and offer alternatives to your "dialog."

Once you understand these profiles, you can create or redesign a Web site that appeals to your visitors' needs and helps persuade them as they most like to be persuaded. Knowing who your visitors are is going to influence everything you do on your Web site, from how you structure your selling process, to how and where you place different categories of information, what calls to action you provide, how you write your copy, and even the colors you choose.

It really is that important.

AIDAS Provides the Momentum

AIDAS is an acronym that stands for Attention, Interest, Desire, Action and Satisfaction. In order to work - that is, to move your visitors to and through the close - every one of your Web pages must grab their attention, hold their interest, stimulate their desire to continue the process, motivate them to act (i.e., click and, ultimately, do what you want them to do in a way that makes it feel right to them), and then satisfy them once they've taken the action you've motivated them to take.

As we mentioned earlier, you need to think about conversion from two perspectives. At the macro-level there is the overall conversion goal - purchasing a product or service, subscribing to a newsletter. But a single macro-conversion is made up of a series of steps, each of which represents a micro-conversion - your visitor is successfully persuaded to click through to the next step of the process.

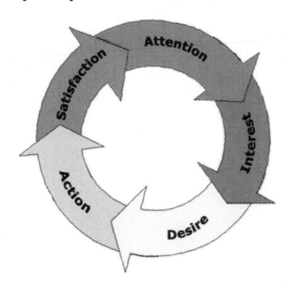

At both the macro- and micro-level of conversion, metrics help you evaluate the efficacy of your process. Commerce metrics provide completion information at the macro-level. Content metrics help you understand the micro-level, or how your visitors are behaving on your site every step of the way. And again, your Single Page Access Reports will illuminate those places where you have short-changed AIDAS.[7]

AIDAS is not simply some business school buzzword. It provides the momentum that keeps your visitors moving through your site, to and through the act of buying. If you don't use it, you have little, if any, control over where your visitors go or why they go there. On the other hand, if you use AIDAS correctly, it will increase your sales directly and immediately.

Every single page of your Web site, every navigation path you establish, should pass The AIDAS Test:

A   Grab their ATTENTION.

Does the page capture them in 10 seconds or less? With something that speaks to their felt needs? And, do you sustain their attention by responding to their clicks (their questions) just as well, just as fast?

I   Strengthen INTEREST.

Do you show your visitors immediately that you can meet their needs? Do you provide useful information in a user-friendly format? Do you give them a reason to stay? Do you make it easy for them to find everything they are looking for?

D   Stimulate DESIRE.

Inspire your visitors to stay with you and keep clicking up to and through the close. Ignite and fan the flames of their desire by appealing to benefits rather than features; in doing this, you offer a compelling portrait of the value of your product or service that appeals at an emotional level.

---

[7] For more information on metrics, refer to pages 154-156.

A   Get them to take ACTION.

The action you want them to take may mean making a purchase, or it may mean ensuring they click again on the path toward a purchase. It might involve getting them to register, subscribe, opt-in or generate referrals. Whatever action you are trying to motivate, make it logical, easy, obvious, desirable and safe - even for a newbie. Do you lead your visitors through the buying process in a way that makes sense to them? Are you helping them to take action, pushing them to take action, or demanding they take action? Which would you prefer as a customer experience?

S   SATISFY them.

Does every click on every page get them more of what they want? Or do some clicks get them what you want to push, or confuse them, or display what one of your programmers or graphic artists wanted to show off? Do some clicks generate error messages? Does the experience of interacting with your site delight your customers? Does it make them feel good about doing business with you? Satisfied customers complete their transactions. Delighted customers come back and tell others. Dissatisfied people don't come back and tell even more people about their bad experiences.

Navigation Provides the Lubrication

If AIDAS provides the momentum for your visitors to keep moving toward the close, good navigation provides the lubrication, making it easy for them to do so. It must be simple, clear and intuitive. It must respect their expectations and conventions (e.g., hyperlinks - and nothing else - should be blue and underlined). And it must be consistent from page to page. Otherwise you are asking your visitors to learn your new methods rather than shop. Even if they try - and most won't - the minute they get confused and frustrated, they will leave. Navigation is no place to get clever; it will only cost you sales.

FOR EXAMPLE

Web sites employ a variety of navigation strategies, but most fall into three general categories: global navigation, comprehensive navigation and local navigation. These are the lists that typically appear across the top of a Web page, or in columns along the side.

One of the most effective ways you can help your visitors navigate your Web site is through hyperlinking specific text phrases in your copy. Text hyperlinks allow you to target the different personalities who visit your site and perform the invaluable function of keeping your visitors fully engaged in the "active window," the real estate of your Web page that is most intensively focused on the conversion process. It's important to understand that any time your visitor disengages from the conversion process - to use the browser buttons to relocate, to search for peripheral information in supplemental areas of your screen - you risk losing that visitor.

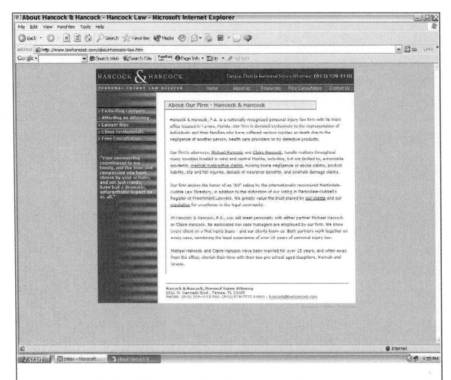

The active window (the central white area) of Hancock & Hancock's About Us Web page contains text that is formatted for scanning and skimming and includes standard, blue-underlined hyperlinks targeting information that will appeal to different personality types. Using these links, visitors can navigate the site without having to disengage from the active window to use left-column or top-bar navigation.

Putting It All Together

When we work with clients, we focus on five discreet areas where improvements can be made to increase conversion rates: Planning, Structure, Momentum, Communication and Value.

Planning

Planning ideally takes place before your visitors reach your site. This includes everything from how you are going to get traffic, to developing your UVP (Unique Value Proposition), planning the elements for the wireframe and storyboard of your site, understanding your marketplace, your visitors, your brand and positioning, your strengths and weaknesses, and more. It's also about understanding everything your visitors went through before they got to your site, so you can anticipate their knowledge levels, moods and mind sets.

Your organization needs to understand the interdependent but distinct roles of Marketing and Sales. Before your potential customers arrive at your web site, they are exposed to numerous external messages. Mentally, they compare those messages to their internal desires and values. This is where marketing plays an important role in creating the inclination to visit your site and the propensity to buy what you are selling or take whatever other action you desire.

But do not confuse marketing with sales - they are not the same! Marketing paves the way for sales. However, it's only where sales (professional persuasion) and marketing (the ability to deliver qualified visitors) overlap that buying happens. As soon as your visitors begin to interact with your "digital store," all the marketing in the world isn't going to sell them if your site doesn't know how to convert them. And if your remedial response to poor results is based on spending more money to drive more traffic instead of working to increase the conversion rate of the traffic you already get, then you are literally sending your marketing dollars up in smoke.

To be most effective, your marketing and sales messages and methods must be congruent. Unfortunately, most companies do not have a single person who is "directly responsible" for the "sales effectiveness" of the company Web site. If you can help change that, you will be doing your company a huge service.

Structure

Improving the structure of a Web site includes analyzing and evaluating the effectiveness of many elements: Navigation, Information Architecture, Design/Style (Look/Feel), Color, Text versus Images, Layout, Technology, Font (size, style, color), Usability, raw Speed, as well as the perception of speed and much more. This is where understanding your site's "sales metrics" can help you determine which parts of your site structure need help.

Momentum

Momentum considers the elements that motivate people to go from one page to the next and eventually to take action on your site. Some of the main elements that can be improved in Momentum include:

- AIDAS
- The 5-Step Sales Process

For Example

Reports of navigation activity paths, in combination with detailed conversion rate metrics, can help you identify which products or services your visitors buy most frequently. This is essentially an application of the Pareto Principle or the 80/20 Rule: you typically find 20% of your visitors account for the sale of 80% of your products or services. With this information in hand, you can design your conversion process so it quickly gets your visitors to the products they most likely want. It also helps you devise effective merchandizing strategies, such as bundling.

After reviewing traffic and conversion patterns for MagMall, we created best-seller lists of the magazines people purchased most often, as well as magazine bundles, and featured these on the home page, separate from the global and comprehensive navigation schemes. These changes took MagMall's overall conversion rate from 1.21% to 4.93% - an increase of more than 400%.

- Calls to Action - Make sure every page has a clear one. If you want your visitors to do something, don't just hope they'll figure it out. Tell them (e.g., "Click Here").
- Optimizing your Active Window to serve as the primary area of activity, including navigation.
- Usability and Beyond - Usability is essential, but all it does is remove obstacles to buying. You have to go beyond usability to actually create the desire for your product or service and then motivate the action of purchasing.
- Get The Cash - (Get The Click - get the result you want.)
- POA (Point of Action) - Make sure you locate items on your site at the places where they will have the most impact by speaking to what is in your customers' minds at that point in the sales process. Example: putting your guarantee policy on your home page is premature; not putting it on your checkout page is a big mistake.
- Paralysis of Analysis - People get overwhelmed by too much information and too many choices. Don't try to convey every aspect of your business on one page, and keep your customers' choices to the minimum that balances opportunity with overload.

Communication

The Internet is nothing more or less than a very powerful, very fast and very flexible communication tool, with the potential to be very effective. Communicating effectively involves monitoring and improving your writing, evaluating your use of images versus copy, expressing value, setting the appropriate mood, developing policies and procedures that instill trust, selling style or substance, timing your messages for best effect, formatting your copy for scanning and skimming, effectively managing your follow-up communication, knowing when you should use long or short copy, and more.

Far too many sites invest more time, talent and money in design than in copy, without realizing their money would be better spent the other way round. Numerous studies prove the words you use have the greatest impact online. Do you speak in language your visitors understand, or is your site full of jargon? Can you recognize and address different personality types, selling different visitors in the way they want to be sold? Do you talk about yourself or them?

FOR EXAMPLE

Communicating is, in large part, about what you say. But it is also about how you present your information. Ideally, you want to format text so your visitors can quickly scan and skim for attention-grabbing, relevant material. Bolding, headlining, highlighting, employing sufficient white space, keeping paragraphs short and to the point - these are some of the techniques that help keep the reader engaged with your copy, which enhances your ability to communicate and improves your conversion rates.

Sedona.com has a healing mission and a lot to say about that mission, which means they have a very text-rich site. Much of our work with this client centered around identifying the key headlines that would grab a visitor's attention, then making those headlines visually pop from the page. The number of leads Sedona gets has doubled.

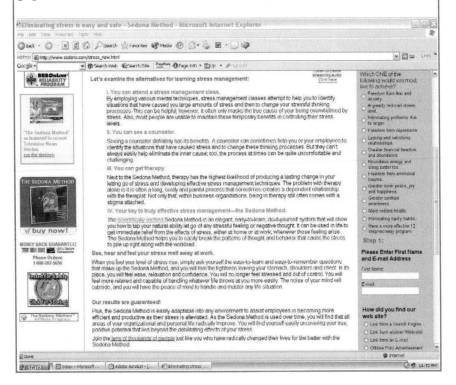

Finally, ask yourself: do you know what you are really communicating to your visitors? Communication is not what we intend, it is always and only what the recipient perceives. Objective evaluation of your "message" is essential. Having an outside party create or review your communication will pay for itself many times over.

Value

Your ability to express to your visitors the value of your products or services and the value of doing business with you ultimately determines whether your "visitors" will turn into "customers." Are you effective at selling your benefits rather than features - speaking to what your customer wants to buy instead of what you want to push? Is the style of your site consistent with your USP? Do you delight customers with fulfillment of their orders, or do you merely satisfy or, even worse, disappoint them? Do your site's products and services, as well as the text that describes them, address your customers' deeply felt needs? Remember, value is not the same as price, and price alone is actually quite low on most buyers' lists of priorities.

The Brain's Behind It All

The brain is a fascinating place, and understanding some of the ways in which it functions and processes information can greatly benefit your online persuasion tactics.

Few advertisements, on- or offline, actually produce exceptional results. Remember the Nissan TV commercials with G.I. Joe™ and Barbie™ jumping into his car? They had outstanding viewer recognition, but sales spiraled downward at an incredible rate. The "creative" thinking behind that series ignored how the human mind works. And undertakings that don't respect the workings of the brain are likely to fail.

If we're going to pursue an activity that not only engages the brain but also, hopefully, motivates a specific action, it would help to know a little about how the brain works in these affairs.

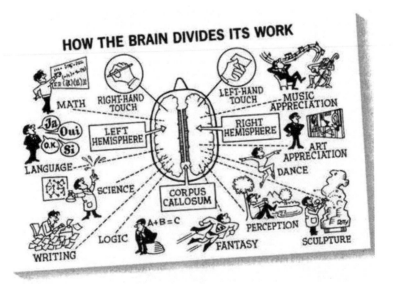

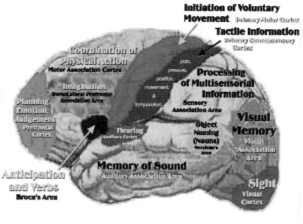

Initiation of Voluntary Movement *Primary Motor Cortex*

Tactile Information *Primary Somatosensory Cortex*

Coordination of Physical Action
Motor Association Cortex

Imagination
DorsoLateral Prefrontal Association Area

Planning, Emotion, Judgement
Prefrontal Cortex

Processing of Multisensorial Information
Sensory Association Area

Hearing
Auditory Cortex

Object Naming (Nouns)
Wernicke's Area

Visual Memory
Visual Association Area

Memory of Sound
Auditory Association Area

Anticipation and Verbs
Broca's Area

Sight
Visual Cortex

Concept by: Silvia Helena Cardoso, PhD
Center for Biomedical Informatics, University of Campinas, Brazil

Brain Map Review – Wizard of Ads Academy

Surprising Broca

> *We tried to find out what people think of advertising ... whether the advertising community was loved by the American people. We're not even hated! They ignore us. So the most important thing as far as I'm concerned is to be fresh, to be original.*
>
> William Bernbach

Roy Williams has been providing valuable strategies and insights to his clients for a number of years. According to him, success in advertising is all about "surprising Broca" - nudging that part of the human brain (Broca's Area) that makes comprehensible order out of the input it receives.

In 1861 Paul Broca identified the section of the brain involved in speech production. It assesses the syntax of words while listening to and understanding what is structurally very complex. The brain does its job by learning rules about how we talk and then, based on those rules, learns to skip over the parts of what we hear that we expect to encounter. "The listener [or reader] uses Broca to anticipate and discount the predictable." In other words, if humans hear or read exactly what they expect to hear or read, it doesn't impress them - it doesn't capture their attention. "To gain Broca's smiling approval and win [your audience's] attention ... you must electrify Broca with the thrill of the unexpected."[8]

[8] *Accidental Magic.* Roy Williams. Bard Press, 2001. p 16.

When you think about it, it seems obvious. We are drawn to things that are surprising, shocking, catastrophic, and chaotic. Anything predictable is boring. And research indicates these surprises imbed themselves in memory. Back to the G.I. Joe™ and Barbie™ ad, which at least effectively surprised Broca. Lots of people remember the story line, how the ads were filmed, even the Van Halen music. But very few remember which car the ad was promoting.[9]

How Visual Are We Really?

We read everywhere, and are reminded by graphic designers, that advertisers need to remember we are visual beings. While we may be bombarded with more visual marketing stimuli than ever before, to say that because we're being buried in visual images we're visual beings is like saying because we periodically fill ourselves up with air we're balloons. We aren't nearly as visual as people assume. "Going visual" is not the cure-all that will allow you to connect more effectively with your audience.[10]

Sound is a far more effective medium than sight for conveying information, affecting emotions and motivating action. Here's something to try at home: First watch your TV with the sound off, then listen to your TV with the picture off. You can prove to yourself in just seconds, for free, with no fancy research (although there's plenty of good research out there if you want it), that sound beats sight hands down.

The reason sound is far more effective than pictures in causing people to take action lies in the physiology of the brain. At the front of the brain, right behind your forehead, is the prefrontal cortex, which is the center for planning, emotion, and judgment. Its job is to give the signal to the adjacent motor association cortex to coordinate behaviors, and then initiate voluntary movement (take action). Until your messaging has reached the prefrontal cortex, all you have done is take up space and make noise.

The shortcut into the human brain is the ear. The auditory cortex is right next door. Raw sound enters the auditory cortex, and spoken words, melodies, rhythm, laughter, and jingles are stored in the auditory

---

[9] The principal problem with the campaign lay not in its inability to surprise Broca, which it did in spades, but in the unfortunate decision to promote style over substance with a big-ticket item very few people purchase for style alone.

[10] The Sanford-Poynter studies demonstrated that in the online environment, users actually engage with text before they examine pictures. And sometimes, they don't even bother to look at the pictures at all. Online, copy has priority.

association area. That's why you can remember hundreds of songs you never intended to learn ("You deserve a break today at ...").

Robin Frederick, one of the premier music producers in the field of family entertainment, writes,

> I am a big proponent of fantasies. After all, everything in life starts with an idea - from a Fortune 500 company to a great painting to a romantic fantasy. Ideas become reality when we put energy into them, especially emotional energy. Studies have shown that the emotion accompanying an idea or image causes it to realize itself- the more emotion, the more quickly the idea becomes reality. By using music to evoke emotions, you give your fantasy a passionate, single-minded energy that can propel it right into your life. Or, as Billy Ocean once put it, "... outta my dreams and into my car."

> Like some mythological beast - half speech, half music - songs have a seemingly magical power to revive long-forgotten memories and give voice to our deepest feelings. In fact, songs speak directly to some of the most primitive parts of the brain, evoking deeply-felt emotional responses, triggering involuntary recall of events, and conveying powerful messages while essentially bypassing the rational, analytical areas of the mind.

> The Inner Critic is that little voice that believes you do not deserve abundant love, good health, or success. But this is only the opinion of one part of your brain - your judgmental, analytical, rational left brain. There is a whole area of your brain that doesn't make judgments at all, and it is here that songs are processed and make their deepest impression.

> Although the ability to speak and form thoughts into words and sentences rests almost exclusively with the left side of the brain, the understanding of the emotional tone of voice is a function of the right side. Thus both sides of the brain are needed to correctly interpret the content of spoken words, with most of that activity taking place on the left side. But when these same words are sung, the left/right division of labor shifts dramatically. Lyrics are absorbed and processed almost exclusively in the "non-verbal" right hemisphere. In fact, neurologists have reported that when the left hemisphere of the brain is sedated (or damaged), the

subject is unable to speak but can still sing words. If the right hemisphere is impaired, the person can speak normally but cannot sing (Anthony Storr, Music and the Mind). In songs, then, the right hemisphere is handling the verbal information rather than the normally dominant left hemisphere.

Now, there's a funny thing about the right side of your brain - it is not concerned with making judgments or assessing the factual truth of a statement; that's the left brain's job. And there's yet another way in which song lyrics can sneak their message past your Inner Critic... Good poets make extensive use of "right-brain language". Forget that sensible, linear, factual left-brain speech. The language of the right brain is a horse of a different color. A riot of imagery, a cascade of connections, sensations, and associations. The right brain speaks in metaphors, juxtapositions, and similes, using a whole range of poetic devices to express the inexpressible and describe the indescribable. Emotions? No problem. Hearts soar. Lips taste like wine. Eyes are mirrors of the soul. Imagine what your left brain thinks of that. Utter nonsense! Not worth even bothering about! But to your illogical, intuitive right brain, it's perfectly clear.[11]

According to cognitive neuroscience, our thoughts are composed of neither words nor pictures. Human thought is a speed-of-light progression of mental images, each one a complex composite of sound, shape, texture, color, smell, taste, and mood. Different words are attached to these mental images in an area of the brain called Wernicke's Area. This is the area responsible for naming, for associating nouns with objects. Once a word has been attached to each mental image, the whole verbal jigsaw puzzle moves to Broca's Area, where the words are arranged into understandable patterns.

The problem for advertisers is that when Wernicke's Area attaches the "usual" words and Broca's Area arranges them in the "usual" order, the result can be painfully predictable and, therefore, eminently forgettable. Only when you break the pattern of predictability do you achieve impact and memorability.

[11] "Reality Begins with Imagination." Robin Frederick. Appearing in *Magical Worlds of the Wizard of Ads: Tools and Techniques for Profitable Persuasion.* Roy H. Williams. Austin: Bard Press. 2001. pp 20-21.

Where is the sound in your writing?

It's in the words, which we "hearing" in our minds.

Roy Williams writes that the secret of persuasion lies in the skillful use of action words: "The magic of advertising is in the verbs ... Describe what you want the listener to see, and she will see it. Cause her to imagine taking the action you'd like her to take, and you've brought her much closer to taking the action."[12]

Sound is invasive, intrusive, and irresistible. Driving sound through Broca's Area allows us to cross the bridge to the dorsolateral prefrontal association area, otherwise known as the imagination.

So what does this mean for your online efforts? It means you will be most successful when you use words that allow your message to cross from the ear almost directly to the prefrontal cortex, the decision part of the brain. Verbs. Dynamic-action verbs. Bottom line: The killer app is not sight, it's sound, whether heard directly (audio) or mentally (read through copy).

Electrical versus Chemical Memory

If you want to capture a share of your audience's mind, it helps to understand something about how memory works.

Electrical memory is short-term. It's the thought you are thinking right now ... no, right now ... get it? It's imagination, the ability to see possibilities in your mind. It is temporary by nature; the RAM of the human computer that is your brain.

When you go to sleep, your brain powers down, and most of what is in electrical memory gets lost during the nighttime (as when a PC is switched off and short-term memory, RAM, disappears). Sleep causes the information in electrical memory to fade according to its relevance. More important information doesn't fade as fast as the trivial stuff.

Electrical memory is of limited capacity. If you try to add an item to it, the new item pushes out a previous, less-relevant one. Imagine aiming a fire hose at a teacup. All the information coming at you - TV, radio, Web pages, newspapers, emails, billboards, direct mail, fliers, music, plus what your kid swapped her peanut butter and jelly sandwich for at school - is the water consistently and vigorously trained on the teacup (a.k.a. your brain, or, more specifically, your electrical memory). Some of the water stays in the teacup; the rest spills out. Relevance determines which "water

---

[12] *Monday Morning Memo*. Roy H. Williams. http://www.wizardacademy.com.

drops" stay in - you store in electrical memory only the information that's important to you at a certain moment in time.

Once you get a message to stay inside the teacup, the human computer works on transferring it from electrical to chemical memory.

Chemical memory is long-term, stored memory ... it's everything you can remember. It's the equivalent of your computer's hard disk. If you really need to store your data so you can get it back, you save it to the hard disk before you power down your computer. Unlike the ephemeral RAM of electrical memory, chemical memory is the repository of "known information" from the hard drive of the human computer.

Chemical memory, business-wise, is "top of mind awareness;" it is being the company your customers think of first and feel best about whenever they need your products or whenever your product category is named (in other words, branding).

Businesses try to "whip people into action" with the urgency of a limited-time offer. They can be sure at best, that if their message is relevant, it will stay in electrical memory only until the expiration date, after which it will be erased forever from the brain.

When a business focuses effort on limited-time offers, the only thing that makes it into chemical memory is: "this business makes limited-time offers." In essence, the business is training the customer to ask, "When does this go on sale?"

Three things can be done to speed the transfer of a message from electrical memory to chemical memory:

- Increase the relevancy of the message
- Increase the frequency of its repetition
- Increase both the relevancy of the message and the frequency of its repetition

Branding is accomplished only when you have a relevant message that is repeated with enough frequency to become securely stored in chemical memory.

Buy-now messages are immediate, direct response-type messages by nature, while build-identity messages are aimed at meeting deeper, more long-term goals. It is possible (although not always desirable) for you to do both. You can convey, in the same email communication for example, a powerful, long-term branding message accompanied by one or more short-term, direct response messages.

Few e-commerce companies have valuable or memorable newsletters because they are focused largely on delivering short-term, buy-now messages. Amazon.com understands and takes advantage of the nature of human memory: while many of their messages are buy-now, they cleverly acknowledge people might not remember or act immediately on the message. Their hedge against this is the "add to wish list" option embedded in their emails.

Think unpredictable. Think aural. Think chemical. Armed with even the most cursory of understandings of brain mechanics, you can perform magic.

Testing, Measuring and Optimizing

No matter how good your conversion rate may be, there is always room for improvement. However, maximizing your conversion rate is not simply a matter of making changes, it's about making a) the right changes, b) at the right time, c) in the right sequence, and then d) evaluating the results before continuing the process. With our own clients we have seen that even when a complete redesign is called for, you can make simple improvements in the interim that will have a dramatic affect on your conversion rate - we call this "picking the low-hanging fruit."

Even if they all seem necessary, changes need to be made individually so you can track the result of the change effectively. While you might institute several changes and see an improvement, it could be a "net" improvement - that is, a five percent improvement could be the result of Change One helping ten percent, while Change Two actually hurt by five percent. If you make one change at a time and then discover it doesn't help, it's easier to back up and try something else. If you are not methodical in your approach to change, much of your effort will be wasted. Take your time; in the long run, it will be worth it.

Using commerce and content metrics appropriately should be a critical part of your optimization effort. If you want to have common measures and comparable e-metrics, standard terms are a must. And if you want to communicate clearly about the fruits of your success and the lessons of your setbacks, recognizing standard measurements is imperative. To that end, it's important to consider these issues about metrics and tracking:

+ Make sure your business has standard internal definitions, and stick with them. How you define a page view may be a topic of discussion in your company, but, once you define a page view, stick with the definition. If you change the definition over time, you will essentially be comparing apples to oranges with your metrics and will have difficulty figuring out where you are. This leads into the second issue:

♦ Because you will be making powerful decisions based on your metrics, consistency and accuracy are very important in creating them. But in some cases, you simply cannot get a completely accurate result. However, the potential inability to get an accurate picture of a particular activity does not invalidate the analysis; it simply calls for a different perspective: looking at your trends.

It is possible to obsess too much about finding an absolute answer, when a relative answer can be just as insightful - "Is it getting better or worse?" An absolute number ("we had 449, 963 visitors last week") may not be as important as the relative number ("the number of visitors dropped by 10% last week"). Even if you know there are inaccuracies in a specific number, as long as you calculate the number the same way each time, these inaccuracies will tend to smooth themselves out over time. In some cases you will find you are not really interested in a specific number, but how that number changes over time. Tracking your trends will prove invaluable to evaluating the success of your conversion efforts.

♦ Make sure you always specify a time frame in your analysis. For any given metric, the value of the metric can and does change over time. You can report your sales per visitor is 33 cents, but it doesn't provide much useful information unless you know whether the figure represents average annual sales, sales for June or sales since the beginning of time. Make it clear to people using your reports what the time period of the measurement is. And of course, whenever you calculate your metrics, make sure you are using equal time measurement periods. For example, to calculate sales per visitor, use numbers that represent your sales for a specific time period and the number of visitors for the same time period. Always make sure you are using equal time periods when creating ratios, percentages, and indexes.

- There are many different ways to set up a web site, and the technology used will determine the kinds of data available for analysis. The ability to create any one metric depends greatly on the ability to collect the right data. For example, on the content side, the site may not be able to distinguish a Unique Visitor. On the commerce side, many commerce systems focus on orders rather than customers, and lack the capability to distinguish between an order from a new customer and an order from a current customer. We encourage you to focus the analysis on unique visitor or customer level data whenever possible.

Key Conversion Metrics[13]

Content Metrics	Commerce Metrics
Defining Visitor Activity	Converting Activity into Profits
Take Rates: Newsletter, Bookmarks, Downloads	Average Order Amount (AOA)
Repeat Visitor Share	Conversion Rate (CR)
Heavy User Share	Sales per Visit (SPV)
Committed Visitor Share	Cost per Order (CPO)
Committed Visitor Index	Repeat Order Rate (ROR)
Committed Visitor Volume	Cost Per Visit (CPV)
Visitor Engagement Index	Order Acquisition Gap (OAG)
Reject Rate: All Pages	Order Acquisition Ratio (OAR)
Reject Rate: Home Page	Contribution per Order (CON)
Scanning Visitor Share	Return on Investment (ROI)
Scanning Visitor Index	
Scanning Visitor Volume	

[13] Calculators for these conversion metrics are available as free resources at www.futurenow-inc.com/digitalsalescalculators.htm and are fully explained in *The Marketer's Common Sense Guide to E-Metrics*.

Conversion is Music to Our Ears

When we talk about conversion, some of our clients have difficulty seeing how all the bits and pieces interrelate. One day the three of us were in the car on a long drive to a client meeting. We got to talking about music, and through a series of brainstorms, one thing led to another. The result was a musical metaphor for understanding the complexity of conversion as a system.

It's a satisfying framework that appeals to both the right and the left brain, and it has helped any number of our students and clients grasp the bigger picture. We hope it works for you!

Imagine conversion is a musical composition.

WIIFM: The Bass Line

At the most fundamental level, every user is motivated by the question, "What's in it for me?" (WIIFM). This is like a bass line - the perceived undertone that grounds the user at all times. In our musical score, think of WIIFM as the musical foundation which deliberately moves the listener (the reader of your email or the visitor to your Web site) toward an ending that is satisfying, delightful and feels complete.

Failure to address WIIFM throughout your composition is the single element most likely to interfere with a higher conversion rate. Your prospects' motivations change by individual personality type, mood, environment, intelligence, expertise in your product or service, level of experience with the Web and other psychographic factors. By virtue of their complex natures, humans introduce an element of chaos (as a non-random system) that will always thwart total predictability.

The goal of a good conversion system is to support a maximum degree of flexibility and acknowledge as many of these personal and psychological variables as possible throughout the structure and design of the site.

AIDAS: The Beat

On top of the bass line and presenting an organizing rhythm, our musical score adds AIDAS (Attention, Interest, Desire, Action and Satisfaction), the beat that propels the user through the goal of conversion.

To maintain this momentum, your copy must grab your prospect's attention and stimulate an interest in moving forward. This is an iterative process. You create and nurture your prospect's desire for the product or service until the decision to take action occurs, all the while making certain the entire experience is satisfying. The ability of the rhythm to draw your prospect in, keep your prospect focused and move your prospect along the process requires you to pay attention to every element in the design and execution of your email and your Web site. The second the rhythm falters, your visitors disengage with the process. This is typically when they will decide to bail out.

5-Step Sales Process: The Melody

The tune, the component of our composition that is easiest to grasp and the one to which the listener will most consciously pay attention, is the 5-step sales process of Prospect, Rapport, Qualify, Present and Close.

Online, the melody begins with prospecting (marketing tactics that deliver qualified visitors). Once your visitors arrive, you immediately undertake developing rapport, which communicates your company understands their needs and can meet them in a manner that isn't just satisfying, but delightful. Through the iterative experience of qualifying and presenting, your email and Web site help your customers clarify exactly what they need and suggest avenues for how they can achieve that need, until your customer is prepared to take the action you want.

The Buying Decision: The Harmony

A bass line and a melody line sound good, rhythm keeps you anticipating, but it's the harmony that completes the effect. Beyond being sensitive to the sales process, your conversion system must also be sensitive to how people make the decision to buy. Always keep in mind that buying is the compliment to selling.

Planning and Execution: The Mechanics of Notation

It isn't apparent to the listener, nor should it be, but from a completely structural perspective, the musical composition has a score. There are staves to which different voices are assigned, a key signature and a meter. In our metaphor, these building blocks that allow the music to be created and communicated, and define its characteristics, are the equivalent to the structural features that allow your visitors to interact easily with your Web site.

And the notes? They constitute the path the music is to take. On your Web site and in your email, these are the planned paths of micro-actions that lead to the culmination of a macro-action.

People intuitively understand music as a coherent whole. If a phrase is omitted, we may not be musicians and able to say why, but the music feels incomplete (it actually can be seen in scans of the brain - showing Broca was surprised). Nor do we have to be musicians to experience the anxiety of dissonance and discordance, or feel disappointment at the absence of a satisfying resolution.

If you ignore parts of the natural melody line you'll leave your listener stranded. If you stray far from the melody line, you'll leave your listener confused. All are frustrating experiences for the user, who will likely get up and walk out on your concert!

All the components of your site must reinforce each other so the result sounds rich and full. If you pay attention to the details, you'll have your listeners' rapt attention. Otherwise, at best, you'll just be background noise.

RESOURCES

Web

ClickZ. Content and Creativity Articles including: Content Development, Publishing, ROI Marketing, Site Design, The Creative Message and Writing Online. Email Marketing Articles. http://www.clickz.com.

Excess Voice. Newsletter and Web site. Nick Usborne. http://www.nickusborne.com.

Got Copy? Newsletter and Web site. Stevie Ann Rinehart. http://members.cox.net/gotcopy/index.html.

GrokDotCom. Newsletter. Future Now, Inc. http://www.grokdotcom.com

I-Copywriting. Discussion List. Adventive (moderated by Nick Usborne). http://www.adventive.com/lists/icopywriting/summary.html.

Wizard Academy. Seminars. Roy H. Williams, Williams Marketing. http://www.wizardacademy.com.

WordBiz. Newsletter and Web site. Debbie Weil. http://www.wordbizreport.com.

WordsToTheBank.com. Website. Future Now, Inc. http://www.wordstothebank.com

Books

The Online Copywriter's Handbook: Everything You Need to Know to Write Online Copy That Sells. Robert W. Bly. Contemporary Books. 2002.

How to Make Friends and Influence People. Dale Carnegie. Reissue edition. Pocket Books. 1994.

The Craft of Copywriting. Alastair Crompton. London: Hutchinson Business. 1987.

The Copy Book: How 32 of the World's Best Advertising Writers Write Their Advertising. Designers and Art Directors Association of the UK, Editors. Rotovision. 2000.

The Analogy Book of Related Words: Your Secret Shortcut to Power Writing. Selma Glasser. Communication Creativity. 1990.

Ogilvy on Advertising. David Ogilvy. New York: Vintage Books. 1987.

Advertising Secrets of the Written Word: The Ultimate Resource on How to Write Powerful Advertising Copy from One of America's Top Copywriters and Mail Order Entrepreneurs. Joseph Sugarman. Las Vegas: DelStar Books. 1998.

Net Words: Creating High-Impact Online Copy. Nick Usborne. New York: McGraw-Hill. 2001.

Accidental Magic. Roy H. Williams, Janet Thomae, Chris Maddock and One Hundred and Six Graduates of Wizard Academy. Austin, Texas: Bard Press. 2001.

GLOSSARY

Above-the-fold
The top portion of an email or web page that is visible without scrolling.

Active Voice
A grammatical property of verbs that indicates a relationship between the subject and the action expressed by the verb. "Birds build nests" is written in the active voice and emphasizes the subject - birds. "Nests are built by birds" is written in the passive voice and emphasizes the action - building nests. Active voice is far more persuasive in driving action.

Active Window
The central portion of computer screen real estate "above the fold" which constitutes the area your visitors are most inclined to focus on. It is the area in which you want to keep the visitor actively engaged in the conversion process at all times.

After Sales
No less a part of the professional selling process than closing the sale, everything that occurs after the "buyer" has taken action must not merely satisfy, but delight. This includes confirmation of the action taken, appropriate follow-up through exceptional fulfillment and opportunities for your customer to offer feedback and participate in viral marketing. The after sales experience of delight can be severely compromised if you fail to honor your promises, particularly those relating to guarantees and privacy.

AIDAS
"Attention, Interest, Desire, Action, Satisfaction" - elements of the conversion message that establish and sustain the prospect's momentum from initial contact up to and beyond the "close."

B2B
An acronym for business-to-business.

B2C
An acronym for business-to-consumer.

Benefits versus Features
Benefits address a prospect's emotional needs and communicate how the product or service will improve his/her quality of life or make him/her feel better. Features address the attributes of the product or service. Benefits are more effective in driving action.

Brochureware
A website that is essentially nothing more than a form of advertising, providing information but failing to actively motivate its visitors through the decision to buy. Any conversion effort that does not capture, engage and motivate its visitors can, at best, only hope those visitors will choose to take action.

Browser Compatibility
The degree to which all displays and functions of the website work correctly in both past and present versions of principal browsers (Internet Explorer, Netscape, AOL, etc.)

Buyer
A lead currently in negotiation who has made a commitment in principle to buy, but has not yet purchased the product or service.

Calls to Action (see also Point of Action - POA)
Words that offer the opportunity and encourage the prospect to take action. For example, "Click here to see CM3's new designer colors" or "Add this product to your wish list."

Click-through
When a prospect takes an action and clicks on a link. Also known as CTR.

Color Theory
A body of knowledge concerning the ability of color to help create an appropriate psychological state and present information most effectively, in addition to engaging prospects and directing their progress through the process.

Conversion

1. A process whereby a visitor is converted into a "buyer" (used in the most general sense of someone who takes the desired action).
2. A system (i.e., Web site) for managing the process of conversion. This system includes not only tactics for persuading the visitor to take action, but also incorporates mechanisms for tracking the flow of traffic through the conversion process, so that areas needing improvement can be easily identified.

Conversion Rate

The key metric to evaluate the effectiveness of a conversion effort, reflecting the percentage of people converted into buyers out of the total population exposed to the conversion effort. For Web sites, the conversion rate is the number of visitors who took the desired action divided by the total number of visitors in a given time period (typically, per month). For email marketing, the conversion rate is the number of people who take an action divided by the total number of people who received the email. (Multiply these numbers by 100 to express the results as percentages.)

Customer

A person or organization who has paid for your product or service. In broader usage, a customer is one who has indicated an interest in what you offer, by taking an action you have motivated either on your Web site or via your email (opting-in, registering, subscribing, establishing an account, etc.).

Customer Experience

The customer's (possibly only the prospect's) overall experience of pleasure during the sales encounter.

Customer Service

Both online and offline, a business must be available to respond to its visitors' concerns, frustrations and questions with service that is not merely satisfying, but delightful. Options include offering a fax number, a toll free number, email contact and online help (FAQ and information boxes). Whenever possible, customer service issues should always be handled in a personalized manner, ideally by a human rather than an autoresponder.

Delight Factor

The degree to which the overall experience leaves the customer feeling it is worth repeating and worth telling others about.

Font

A complete set of type of one style and size. For example, all the characters associated with 12 point Arial constitute a font.

Fulfillment

Everything that makes up timely and delightful delivery of the product or service, including confirmations, packaging and presentation, shipping notification, the ability to track shipments, etc.

Get the Cash (GTC)

The sales axiom that describes the business's goal to move the customer toward a completed transaction. In e-commerce, GTC can refer to a completed purchase (get the cash), a completed action such as subscribing or registering (get the customer) or simply getting the visitor to take the next step in the conversion process (get the click).

Graphic versus Text

Speed of page delivery is critical. Slow-loading graphics will frustrate visitors and persuade them to leave. When images are called for, they must appear as quickly as possible on the computer screen. Using thumbnails to speed delivery can be advantageous; using high quality copy that engages your visitor while they are waiting for images can also make the download time seem faster.

Incentive

A reason to take action, which might include discounts, bonuses, free shipping, bundle pricing, etc.

Information Architecture

The layout, organization, labeling, navigation, and searching systems that help people find and manage online information.

Instills Trust

The ability of the online effort to create trust and confidence in the mind of prospects, which increases their propensity to take action.

KISS

"Keep it Simple, Stupid" - a directive to keep the conversion process clear, concise and intuitive to improve the likelihood prospects will take action.

Landing Page

The page on a Web site where the visitor arrives (which may or may not be the home page). In terms of an email campaign, one can think of the landing page as the page to which the email directs prospects via a link. A landing page must satisfy all the requirements pertaining to a home page.

Layout

The arrangement of elements designed to optimize use of screen real estate. Layout may need to take into account the fact that only a small portion of the content will appear in the visible window ("above the fold") or preview pane, and further reading requires prospects to scroll.

Lead

A prospect who is engaged actively in the buying decision for a product or service and has identified him- or herself.

Load Time

The length of time it takes for a page to open completely in the browser window. Generally this is a measure of raw speed, although it is possible to affect the visitor's perception of load time by making sure critical elements that engage attention load first.

Look and Feel

The degree to which design, layout and functionality is appealing to prospects and fits the "image" the business is trying to portray.

Multimedia / Plug-Ins

Using elements on your site that require your visitor to download plug-ins that are not typically a part of their browser will generally encourage them to leave - the visitor must completely disengage from the sales process to perform a technical function. Whenever your visitors disengage from the process, the risk they will simply leave is huge. Even waiting for Flash presentations to appear or media downloads to finish can frustrate visitors. Be sensitive to this issue when you offer these to your visitors: information about file sizes and typical download times can be helpful.

Navigation
The tabs, text and graphic hyperlinks that always let prospects know both where they are and where they can go. Navigation elements must always be available and obvious. Well-designed navigation will lead the prospect in the intended direction.

Paragraph Length (Average)
The average number of sentences in a paragraph, determined by dividing the total number of sentences in a document by the total number of paragraphs. Shorter paragraphs encourage readers to stay focused and move through the document.

Personality
The tone your Web site or email communicates through design elements and content: excited, cheerful, playful, serious, concerned, helpful, etc. The personality of the document should be consistent with the personality of the business and the offer. It should remain consistent throughout any one email and consistent across all emails in a campaign. (For "personality" as it pertains to your prospects, see WIIFM.)

Persuasion Factor
The ability of the copy to persuade the recipient to take action.

Persuasion Process
See Sales Process

Point of Action (POA) (see also Calls to Action)
Specific locations in a presentation that offer the opportunity and encourage the prospect to take action.

Presentation
The manner in which the conversion process describes and displays the products or services.

Privacy
The condition of being free from unsanctioned intrusion. Web sites and emails need to reassure the prospect through clear, accessible and enforced assurances so he/she can feel comfortable about providing personal information and transacting business.

Prospect
A suspect who actively expresses interest in the product or service.

Readability
The degree to which the copy is well-written as well as optimized for reading on the web. The readability of text is affected by many factors including, but not limited to: the color of the text in relation to the background color, the font, the spacing between words and between lines of text, the length of lines of text, how blocky and dense the paragraphs appear, text justification, the complexity of the grammar and the education level of your audience.

Relationship Building
Undertaking strategies and tactics aimed at developing a positive and ideally long-term relationship with the prospect or customer.

Sales Metrics
Parameters that help you evaluate and track the success of your business. While it is the most powerful, Conversion Rate is but one of many sales metrics a business can employ to track the efficiency of the conversion system. For a suite of free downloadable calculators, visit Future Now, Inc. at http://www.futurenowinc.com/digitalsalescalculators.htm.

Sales Process
A multi-step persuasion process that begins with Prospecting (largely a Marketing function), continues through establishing Rapport, Presenting, Qualifying and culminates in the Close. While it is linear to the extent that the Close is the goal, the process itself typically operates in an iterative fashion.

Scannable Text

Highlighted, bolded, bulleted or otherwise visually-distinguished content that allows the reader to quickly scan a web page, orient themselves, and determine if the page contains information of interest.

Security

The ability of the website to communicate to visitors that it is a secure environment, from both a technological and emotional point of view.

Search Engine Optimization

Design and programming - including attention to title, keywords, alt tags and meta tags - that takes into account the ability of the website to place well in search engines and directories.

Sentence Length (Average)

The average number of words in a sentence, determined by dividing the total number of words in a communication by the total number of sentences. In general, shorter sentences capture and retain a reader's interest best. Long sentences can be confusing.

Skimmable Text

Text written in such a way, and perhaps enhanced with bolding or other visible features, that enables the reader to distill the main points and essential features of the communication quickly, allowing them to decide if they want to read the entire thing.

Suspect

Any one individual from the universe of potential customers for the product or service.

Terminology

Words that communicate specifics about the features and benefits of the product or service, or features and benefits of the sales process. Content needs to communicate effectively in language that avoids jargon, does not require insider knowledge and is understood easily. In email campaigns, it is particularly important that terminology avoid clichés and "spam words" such as "free," "limited time offer," etc.

Tools
Websites use a variety of "tools" to enhance the shopping experience. These can include shopping carts, immediate online authorization of credit cards, wish lists, forms, etc. To be beneficial elements in the conversion process, all tools must be efficient, intuitive (and come with help information), and truly helpful.

Tracking
Collecting and evaluating the statistics from which one can measure the effectiveness of an email or an email campaign.

Traffic
People directed to your site through the various marketing and advertising programs a business employs to "drive traffic."

Trust
The condition of having built rapport with your prospects in such a way that they respect your integrity and have confidence you will keep your promises as well as meet, if not exceed, their expectations.

Type
A size or style of typewritten or printed character. For example, a serif type (or typeface), a sans-serif type, 10 point type, 14 point type.

Unique Value Proposition (UVP)
The concise and memorable phrase that concisely and powerfully describes the unique value of your business and creates excitement in the prospect. The UVP is not a slogan or a phrase designed for advertising, although that is one potential use for it. Instead, its purpose is to answer the prospect's implicit question, "Why should I do business with you and not somebody else?"

Up-Selling / Cross-Selling
Presenting customers with an opportunity to purchase related products, services or accessories to products they have shown an interest in or previously purchased.

Usability
The ability to implement effectively the body of knowledge concerning the human-computer interface in order to remove any obstacles impeding the experience and process of online interactions.

Value
The overall appeal and usefulness of the product or service to the prospect. Rarely is value simply a function of price (which typically ranks fourth among purchase considerations).

Viral Design
Elements and functions included in a communication that encourage and allow recipients to pass the offer along to others, thereby leveraging the marketing effort ("tell a friend," "please forward," etc.).

Visual Clarity
A function, in large part, of layout and design: Pages are easy to scan; text and graphics are clear; prospects can find what they are looking for quickly and easily.

Voice
A grammatical property of verbs that indicates a relationship between the subject and the action expressed by the verb. "Birds build nests" is written in the active voice and emphasizes the subject - birds. "Nests are built by birds" is written in the passive voice and emphasizes the action - building nests. Active voice is far more persuasive in driving action. NOTE: "Voice" also can refer to the personality of your business in your emails and on your Web site.

We We Test
Developed by Future Now, Inc., this metric provides a general measure of the degree to which your communication is customer-centered. It compares the number of customer-oriented words (you, your, etc.) in the communication to the number of self- or company-referential words (we, our, I, me, etc.). http://www.futurenowinc.com/wewe.htm.

WIIFM

"What's In It For Me?" This question always underlies and informs a prospect's decision whether to take the suggested action. Beyond addressing the critical value propositions and benefits that will interest prospects, all messaging must accommodate the deeply-felt, emotional needs and take into account the different personality profiles that influence prospects' different shopping styles. (Amiable, Analytical, Expressive and Assertive are our categorizations for the personality profiles - there have been many other representations of these four groups).

Word Length (Average)

The average number of letters in a word, determined by dividing the total number of letters in a communication by the total number of words. Unless meaning is compromised, choose the shorter word over the longer word.

ABOUT THE AUTHORS

Bryan Eisenberg provides the vision for Future Now. His passion for people has led him to careers in teaching, social work, and sales and marketing. Born and raised in Brooklyn, New York, Bryan lives there with his wife Stacey, his beautiful daughter, Hannah (http://www.hannahmichele.com) and his dog DJ, who suffers from ADD (those who know and love Bryan are not surprised he would bond with such an animal). When not tied intravenously to a DSL line, Bryan can usually be found with a perfectly functional camera in hand, taking early morning walks, and reading everything.

Jeffrey Eisenberg is the CEO of Future Now. Although his past business life has taken him to 26 countries, he now stays pretty close to home in Brooklyn. Jeffrey is divorced, loves his stepson, Joey, and lives with Cindy and their two delightfully disturbed canines Kimba and Bambi. When he isn't working, he's buried deeply in a book, exploring history, language, people, ideas and the strange new worlds that exist in his third dimensional reality.

Lisa T. Davis is Chief Cook and Bottle-Washer of Words at Future Now. She also plays esoteric music on equally esoteric instruments from the Middle Ages. Her cat prefers her writing to her playing. Her son prefers saxophone to cornameuse. They say Lisa lives in the backwaters of Maryland, but really she's tucked into the only undiscovered real estate remaining along the northeast metropolitan corridor. Close to the hustle and bustle of urban life, but no broadband.

WHAT IS WIZARD ACADEMY?

Composed of a fascinating series of workshops led by some of the most accomplished instructors in America, Wizard Academy is a progressive new kind of business and communications school whose stated objective is to improve the creative thinking and communication skills of sales professionals, internet professionals, business owners, educators, ad writers, ministers, authors, inventors, journalists and CEOs.

Graduates participate in online discussions and contribute to the weekly newsletters, monthly musepapers and books published by Wizard Academy Press.

Founded in 1999, the Academy has exploded into a worldwide phenomenon with an impressive fraternity of alumni who are rapidly forming an important worldwide network of business relationships.

"Alice in Wonderland on steroids! I wish Roy Williams had been my very first college professor. If he had been, everything I learned after that would have made a lot more sense and been a lot more useful... Astounding stuff."

Dr. Larry McCleary
Neurologist and Theoretical Physicist

"...Valuable, helpful, insightful, and thought provoking. We're recommending it to everyone we see."

Jan Nations and Sterling Tarrant
Senior Managers, Focus on the Family

"Be prepared to take a wild, three-ring-circus journey into the creative recesses of the brain...[that] will change your approach to managing and marketing your business forever. For anyone who must think critically or write creatively on the job, the Wizard Academy is a must."

Dr. Kevin Ryan
President, The Executive Writer

"Even with all I knew, I was not fully prepared for the experience I had at the Academy... Who else but a wizard can make sense of so many divergent ideas? I highly recommend it."

Mark Huffman
Advertising Production Manager, Procter & Gamble

"A life-altering 72 hours."

Jim Rubart

To learn more about Wizard Academy, visit www.WizardAcademy.com or call the academy at (800) 425-4769.

Wizard Academy awards a limited number of full-tuition scholarships each year to journalists and educators, "the world's truest public servants."